Praise for *You Are Radically Loved*

"You Are Radically Loved will gently guide you through surprisingly powerful practices to reclaim your body, energy, and truth."
  —Melissa Urban, bestselling author and founder and CEO of
  Whole30

"Rosie is the true definition of an authentic leader—vulnerable, grounded, courageous, and compassionate. *You Are Radically Loved* will open your eyes and remind you that transformation is possible—through love."
  —Sahara Rose, bestselling author of *Discover Your Dharma* and
  host of the *Highest Self* podcast

"Rosie delivers authentic and practical wisdom that guides us to return to our most essential truth: We are Loved. These teachings are a balm for the feeling of being lost in the world; Rosie's words lovingly guide us toward reclaiming our truth."
  —Tracee Stanley, author of *Radiant Rest* and creator of
  Empowered Life

"Rosie's story inspires us all to be more resilient, realistic, and creative at the same time. Her journey becomes yours through the universal experiences of fear, mistakes, and the road to self-discovery." —Ryan Harris, Super Bowl champion

"*You Are Radically Loved* teaches us how to be the unconditional best friend to ourselves. Rosie is the friend that we all need in our lives to help us realize that we are enough and that we are never alone. Rosie's story is not only inspiring but also teaches us that who we are is exactly who we should be."
    —Mike Bayer, bestselling author of *One Decision* and CEO of
        CAST Centers

"Rosie Acosta is a caring host who keeps looking for how love can matter in the world. It is a joy to be in conversation with her. She is a welcome voice in the next generation."
    —Mark Nepo, author of *The Book of Soul*

"Rosie is an author who has the ability to fill each word on each page of her book with rivers of kindness and vulnerability. You immediately feel less alone! *You Are Radically Loved* is an invitation to love ALL of you in a deep and profound way."
    —Christine Gutierrez, therapist and author of *I Am Diosa*

"In *You Are Radically Loved*, Rosie reminds us that on our journey to self-love we often need a guide with a 'flashlight' brighter than our own. Rosie—with her rare magic blend of vulnerability, honesty, and humor—is that flashlight. If you've ever felt out of place in your life or in the world, this book will help you change your relationship with yourself so that you can live a life full of connection, love, and authenticity."
    —Tracy Middleton, brand director and editor in chief, *Yoga Journal*

"Rosie has lived through a life of adversity; she has the unique talent of helping you to personally transform your whole life through practice and exuding more love."

—Candice Kumai, bestselling author of *Kintsugi Wellness* and host of the *Wabi Sabi* podcast

"With *You Are Radically Loved*, Rosie writes honestly, mindfully, and with purpose. She offers genuine insight on ways that we can feel more radically loved."

—Ethan Nichtern, author of *The Road Home*

"So many of us are in the process of healing our deepest wounds at this moment on the planet. *You Are Radically Loved* is a soothing balm for that process—replete with the wise, girlfriend-next-door vibes of the inimitable Rosie Acosta. Her spiritual insights come from a place of deep realness, personal practice, and an unwavering commitment to the best of all paths—radical love. I am a massive fan of both the author and the book, and will be reading and rereading these love-soaked pages."

—Katie Silcox, bestselling author and founder of The Shakti School

"*You Are Radically Loved* is nectar for your mind, body, and spirit. Wise, funny, and striking in its truth, this book calls us into more honest, whole, and real love within ourselves through both deeply spiritual and practical means. It is a courageous offering to anyone who is determined to love themselves no mat-

ter the depth of hate they've experienced, internalized, or witnessed. It is for those willing and ready to answer the potent call Acosta puts forth within it, a call toward radical (self) love."
—Octavia Raheem, founder of Starshine & Clay Online Meditation and Yoga for Black Women and Women of Color, and author of *Pause, Rest, Be* and *Gather*

"In the pages of *You Are Radically Loved*, you'll feel Rosie guiding you into a journey to uncover your self-love. As she shares her experiences from growing up in the midst of gang violence in East Los Angeles to teaching and speaking all over the world, she inspires us to overcome our challenges and return to our strength, resilience, and love. The gift of her wisdom infuses these pages to enrich our hearts."
—Agapi Stassinopoulos, author of *Speaking with Spirit*

YOU ARE RADICALLY LOVED

A Healing Journey to Self-Love

ROSIE ACOSTA

A TarcherPerigee Book

tarcherperigee

An imprint of Penguin Random House LLC
penguinrandomhouse.com

Most TarcherPerigee books are available at special quantity discounts for bulk purchase
for sales promotions, premiums, fund-raising, and educational needs. Special books
or book excerpts also can be created to fit specific needs. For details, write:
SpecialMarkets@penguinrandomhouse.com.

Hardcover ISBN: 9780593330159
Ebook ISBN: 9780593330166

Printed in the United States of America
1   3   6   7   9   10   8   6   4   2

Neither the publisher nor the author is engaged in rendering professional advice or
services to the individual reader. The ideas, procedures, and suggestions contained in this
book are not intended as a substitute for consulting with your physician. All matters
regarding your health require medical supervision. Neither the author nor the publisher
shall be liable or responsible for any loss or damage allegedly arising from any
information or suggestion in this book.

Dedicated to

my gurus
Chúy and Chucky,
for guiding me to the truth
and to what it means to be radically loved.

CONTENTS

CONTENTS

PART II
BODY

PART III
SPIRIT

CONTENTS

INTRODUCTION

Finding Our Way

At the end of the day, we can endure much more than we think we can.

—FRIDA KAHLO

read once that it takes upward of ten thousand hours to become an expert or master of a skill.* I guess you could say that I was an expert at living in fear. Growing up, I wished I could be anywhere else but where I was. Other people's lives seemed better than mine. Looking outward was easier. What if I had grown up

---

* Gladwell, Malcolm. *Outliers: The Story of Success.* 1st ed., Back Bay Books, 2011.

in a nicer part of town? What if I had a different body? What if I had made different choices? What if I hadn't grown up where I did?

With all those years of study and practice, fear is very much a skill I mastered. It's a voice that begins in my mind that plays out worst-case scenarios. When I'm on my morning run, I worry that someone could run me over. When I'm in bed watching my favorite show, I think about how someone could break in and kill me, my partner, Torry, and the dogs. When I travel, I imagine the airplane crashing even as I dunk my tea bag in hot water and stare at a beautiful sunrise. When I'm sitting outside staring at my orange tree, I catch a glimpse of the cracks in the concrete and think, *The big one could happen any day now.* A tiny surge of electricity runs through my chest as I begin to panic. I say, "Hello there, old friend."

When I'm not thinking about catastrophic events, I'm consulting Dr. Google to see what kind of illness my symptoms are corroborating. I give myself just enough panic to jump out of my chair and say, "I'm having a heart attack." I live my life wondering, *When will the next shoe drop?* It can all end in an instant. These are all valid fears, but I find that they are most prevailing when things are going well.

Here's a sign that your life is going well: You are alive. You are breathing and you are comfortably enjoying this book. Congratula-

tions, you are well on your way to making it through another difficult day of being human. Your life is going well.

Life is hard and, let's be honest, sometimes it can turn quickly.

Waking hours can drag on. Days that move into weeks turn into months. Years pass stealthily as you celebrate big birthdays, anniversaries, and life's fleeting milestones. Then one day, it's over. We spend so much time filling the void of space and time with things, tasks, and lists that, in the grand scheme of life, don't really matter.

This is depressing.

However, putting things into perspective allows you to reach for more of what's important, for things that matter most. It helps us remember what we are doing here. So, how do we discern what matters? Discernment is the ability to recognize and distinguish the difference between two or more things for the purpose of choosing what serves your highest good.

Living a life in constant fear is exhausting.

I learned all about living in fear while growing up in East Los Angeles. It was not your typical palm-tree-lined, Southern California–dreaming scenery. It was normal to hear the latest news of someone getting killed from gang violence, or some innocent bystander dying from the most recent drive-by shooting. It was normal because it happened just outside our door. So much of my worldview was shaped by the normalization of fear.

I also thought everyone broke the law at some point and that being in the juvenile detention system was a rite of passage. I didn't know that there were any other options on the menu. I didn't even know there *was* a menu. Struggling with debilitating panic attacks while taking medication for anxiety and depression was my "normal."

I've come a long way from worrying about gunshots going through our apartment, but sometimes when I'm lurking on people's Instagram pages, I get the same anxiety I did when I was a child. "I'm not posting enough." I go through hundreds of pictures trying to find the right landscape or the right inspirational quote. I've come a long way from worrying about gunshots going through our apartment.

Social media has become such a prevalent part of our lives. We find ourselves living in a world of instant gratification, where our importance and worthiness are based upon clicks and social "likes." We get "inspiration" via quotes and highlight reels at the expense of our own self-worth. We feel lost and unable to feel loved and genuinely connected. In a world where we have been conditioned to believe we are more connected than ever; we have disengaged from our own selves. The fact is that we do matter, and we don't need anyone outside of ourselves to validate that. We allow misinformation into our psyches without thought or question because it appears on YouTube accounts with millions of views and in posts with clickable headlines.

We have been trained to believe the extraordinary to placate our dissatisfaction with the mundane. We feel more separated from each other than ever before. We are more concerned with being right than being kind. I love social media, make no mistake. It is a great tool, just like everything else, for feeling more connection, but I noticed how much it made me focus on what is *not* happening in my life, as opposed to what *is*. It's our duty to discern whether it's serving our highest self or causing a bigger disconnect from who and what we truly are. Becoming acutely aware of how this is affecting us becomes our most vital challenge, helping us identify what afflictions are being activated and why.

Enlightenment Is a Journey

The Yoga Sutras of Patanjali by Sri Swami Satchidananda discusses five major blocks to the path of enlightenment, as understood by both Buddhist and Hindu traditions. These are known as the five afflictions of the mind, or the five kleshas. They are ignorance, egoism, attachment, aversion, and fear of death.

The afflictions are known to build character and make us stronger, but sometimes life just punches you in the face. That's what yoga and meditation are for. I got a black eye once, and it didn't hurt as much as facing my inner fears. Yogic philosophy has been passed down for thousands of years, and it makes as much sense today as it did at any other time in history.

If you are reading this book, you might be trying to affirm something deep within you that you know to be true. You might be yearning for more love; to be loved, to be in love, or to give love. You came to the right place. I am here to tell you that you are not alone. I'm with you. I feel you; I see you, and I've been there too.

I believed all my issues would magically disappear by becoming a super-enlightened yoga teacher. Any trauma, insecurity, or character defects would dissipate in a puffy cloud of sage and the rest would burn away in a hot yoga room. I dreamed that I would curse less, speak softly, and have long, wavy yoga hair. My route to enlightenment would be seamless. I would meditate daily, listen to spiritual books on Audible, and my chakras would be ultra-aligned.

Then the Universe responded: LOL.

I was trying to fit into a spiritual mold that wouldn't work because that's not who I am.

I quickly learned that getting to a place where I liked who I was would take patience, time, and practice—three things I didn't grow up understanding. I am the most impatient person I know, and I am constantly having to start over. What I did learn was that integrating my life experience into my teachings guided me toward a deeper acceptance of who I was without needing to pretend to be someone I'm not. I couldn't change who I was, or where I came from, but I could change what I believed about myself and the world. I could be more open to making mistakes, and I could learn how to discern what served my highest good and the highest vision of my life.

This journey paved the way for me to **know** what radical love truly was, and it is a journey I will detail in this book through stories of what I've been through, as well as insights and exercises to help you on your journey toward deeper understanding, intentional change, and coming home to your true self.

Each of us has a unique story and value, and each of us is radically loved. This may be difficult for someone like me to believe; someone who needed external proof that there is something bigger than the obstacles in my way, that there's a force greater than myself.

Radical Love

Love is the most powerful thing in the Universe. It unites us. Its absence can drive us apart. We live in a world that is constantly being threatened by scarcity, hate, and division, forces that separate us from the truth we all know: that we are radically loved beings.

Love is a verb. It's something that we do. Our initial introduction to love shapes our view of the entire world. Our lives are meant to prime us and teach us to love and to celebrate our unique journeys, despite all the grit. This book is about understanding where radical love shows up in our lives. It's about how our thought patterns and impressions shape our beliefs, fuel our dreams, and pave the way for our spiritual practice. Most of us are fortunate enough that we can make the creative choice to live a radically loved life.

What Are Radical Truths?

The Radical Truths you'll see throughout this book come from the mantras or statements I found when I was able to inquire within. When I was able to get to the truth of what I felt, it gave way to my healing, and it helped me forge ahead. For me, these truths feel true and right. They are anchors. I hope they'll offer you the same comfort and respite in moments of doubt and inspire you to write your own.

Trust the Practice

I will mention the word *practice* several times in this book. Everything in life is a practice—an application or implementation that is repetitive. We are what we do every day. How does this apply to love? If we practice feeling radically loved to

Everything in life is a practice.

the best of our ability, we can ultimately get to a place where we can feel it anytime, anyplace. It takes practice because life is life. Practice gives you the ability to return to the core of who you are, to be at home within yourself, to accept yourself fully as you are. It helps you connect to the wisdom and happiness that exists in the part of you that has been and always will be unstuck.

Writing Out Your Truth

By reading this book, chapter by chapter, and doing the journaling exercises, meditations, movement practices, and daily rituals, you'll begin to recognize your own radical truths. You'll connect with the deepest parts of yourself. Radical self-honesty leads to radical self-love. You'll connect with yourself by writing and reframing your own life story and narrative, so you feel empowered and connected to who and what you truly are—an unstoppable force.

When I was growing up, writing was the only way I could express my true feelings, and I learned that putting them into words made me feel better. I wrote my first book when I was six years old, and it was "published" by my first-grade teacher. Over the school year, our teacher gave the class writing prompts and had us fill in the blanks. We got prompts like "If I had a dream home it would be . . ." and "If I had three wishes . . ." At the end of the year, she bound our answers together and displayed our books for all the parents to see. I still have that book and occasionally, in nostalgic moments, I look at the images I drew as a small child.

Ever since that young age, I've used journaling to establish order in my chaos. Journaling helps me create a sense of connection to something bigger, something that feels grounded on this earth. When I write things down, it no longer feels like my thoughts and feelings are just random ideas floating in the ether. Journaling makes them feel real and validated. It's a way of engaging with my inner strength. I hope you'll keep a journal as you make your way through this book, and I've included reflection questions at the end of each chapter to guide your writing process.

Getting Real

You might not be where you *want* to be or where you *think* you should be, but you are in this moment in time, nonetheless. To the best of your ability, you are safe, secure in your environment, reading this book. When you don't have your basic needs met, however, it is difficult to embark on spiritual pursuits; not because you can't but because your mind will focus on your basic need to feel safe and secure. This has always been my biggest rub with the world of spirituality. Some self-help books discuss connecting to yourself through meditation, yoga, or just plain positive thinking. I had a difficult time finding books I could relate to that focused on the reality of life, social issues, or past/current challenges. I wanted to learn how I could not only help myself but also how I could bring this knowledge and practice to people like the ones I grew up with—people who if you said, "Just think positive," would roll their eyes and give you the finger. They've been raised to believe that a system is designed to keep them from thriving, and in some cases they are right.

We are all different, we have different needs, but at our core, we all know that to change something, we need to change first. We need to be an agent for change, we must think differently, choose what is possible; we must choose our words mindfully and act wholeheartedly.

Change is scary, but it is the only constant you can count on.

Mind, Body, and Spirit

This book is broken into three parts: Mind, Body, and Spirit. To understand ourselves, we must first understand where we come from and how our mind has been shaped. We must understand that our body is the way to move through our feelings. What you feel, you can heal. By connecting to our body, we recognize a certain level of wisdom that lives within us. We then connect to our spirit, or whatever higher power you understand. We acknowledge that spirit is the essence that is you, completely bound and connected to everything living and breathing.

Yoga means union, the unification of mind, body, and spirit. The root, *yuj*, means "to join or yoke." Yoga is the study of paradoxes, how one thing can exist at the same time as the other, like the yin and yang. There's a little yin in the yang and yang in the yin. When I discovered this system and learned about creating a deep sense of connection and balance, everything in my life became clear. Everything touches everything. It's about balancing the whole. The balance I refer to here isn't about holding two things equally. It's about learning to surf the tides of life: to be like water. Water can adapt to any situation.

If you're with me in this and want to connect with the highest parts of yourself and are ready for radical love, come and have a sit with me; a little daylight mystery never hurt anyone.

Let's begin.

PART I

MIND

Each day is an opportunity to start
something new. To see things differently,
to expand beyond our limitations.

CHAPTER 1

YOU ARE RADICALLY SUPPORTED

Radical Truth: Life makes no sense, but you can still find meaning if you try.

A shark in a fish tank grows up to eight inches, but in the ocean, it will grow to eight feet or more. The shark will never outgrow its environment, and the same is true about you. Our environment has a direct impact on how we grow and develop. What we believe, what we achieve, and how we go about achieving it are all dependent on what we've been exposed to. I always knew I would be a product of my environment. I just never imagined I would do anything about it. So, what's radical love got to do with it?

Radical love requires a courage unlike any other. It calls for us to believe in and become devoted to something that keeps us in this world. Devotion to our own self-worth creates a level of self-trust so that we can make better choices and live more fully.

Among the many reasons we practice yoga, mindfulness, and meditation is to cultivate more discernment and to understand ourselves, our choices, and others on a deeper level. We practice so we'll know what to do when we are not on the safe space of our mat or cushion. Feeling safe is the key, and at times our history can keep us from feeling that safety. When we understand **how** our history has influenced our mind and shaped our reality, we can begin to understand **why** we are where we are. If able and willing, we can reframe our thinking, change our internal dialogue and take the necessary action to **change** our lives. We can reframe our thinking and create a different environment even if, for now, it's only internal. We can change our perception and have a clearer understanding of what is best for ourselves, so that we feel more secure and supported in our actions.

What we think, what we say, and what we do matter. If you want to change, it's your responsibility to make that happen.

For me, changing my environment started when I got arrested. I knew that whatever decision I made after that point would set the tone for the rest of my life.

I was fifteen, standing with my public defender in the Eastlake Juvenile courthouse in Los Angeles. My mom sat behind me in the gallery, and I could feel her eyes burning into the back of my neck.

It was 1999. I was a sophomore in high school and awaiting my sentence for trying to steal a cop car. With a simple stroke of a pen, the judge would decide my fate. He was short and stern and flipped endlessly through case folders. He seemed indifferent, like the job was run-of-the-mill that day. He'd judged boys all day long and seemed confused by what I was doing there. I was a girl, all cleaned up, dressed in my mom's nice clothes, and looked nothing like the teenage gangbangers crowding the benches, two of whom I recognized from our neighborhood. He began listing my failures with the enthusiasm of reading a grocery list—the truancy, my previous arrest, my bad grades. I knew he had the power to decide whether I would be another statistic, because up until that point, that's what I was. This moment would determine whether I would live my life in the system or get a chance at creating a better one.

I realized that I didn't want to be sentenced to a life like the ones I had seen so many of my family members, neighbors, and friends live. A product of my socioeconomic inheritance. Growing up in East LA in the 1990s showed me plenty of examples of heartbreak, hopelessness, and despair. Every family on our street and all of my mom's friends had kids in trouble with the law. Every. Single. One.

Standing in that courtroom at fifteen years old, I knew this moment would define who I would be for the rest of my life. I also knew that if I was actually going to do *better*, I would have

We each see the world we are taught to see.

to swim upstream or I'd become another fixture in juvenile hall. I would have to be radical.

We were instructed that we would break for lunch and that I would get my sentence at the end of the recess. I went into the bathroom and splashed cold water on my face. I thought about the worst-case scenarios, which all resulted in the same restricted life. I would go back to my friends and hear the celebratory "Welcome to the club, homie." As much as this scenario matched my environment and even felt normal, I knew in my heart that it wasn't where I wanted to be. Doing what was normal, what was routine wasn't resulting in anything that benefited me. If anything, it had only resulted in problems. We each see the world we are taught to see. Maybe if I could see the world differently, I would be able to see myself differently too.

Cracks in the Foundation

Learning about where you come from is your first foundational step toward creating the framework for your path. Our roots tell us a story about which lessons we are here to learn and how we can use these lessons to create a deeper connection to who we are. Whether our upbringing was pleasant or not can be irrelevant to the way we decide to live our lives, because we *do* get to choose how we live.

Somewhere along the way, you make a decision that takes you off course. In order to make a change, you need to get to the root of the dysfunction. Most often, you must go all the way to the beginning. To learn why your decision-making is out of order, you must go back to the environment where you first developed and what shaped your perception of the world. If you grew up in a fish tank, you don't know any better. You know what you know.

For me, the view of the outside world came in the form of movies, TV shows, and the posters in our garage, which doubled as my uncle's room—a small, dilapidated space where the floors were lined with food crates of *Thrasher* magazines, empty tequila bottles, and oldies records. A collage of images covered one single wall—Guns N' Roses, N.W.A, Kid Frost, *The Doors* movie poster, and a flag for the Los Angeles Raiders. Magazine tear-outs with images of sunsets and bikini-clad women and stickers with sayings like "Live Life Radically, Surf" and "Stay Rad" were what I might later refer to as an unconscious effort to build a vision board.

Radical comes from the Latin adjective *radix*, which means "root." In Southern California, *rad* or *radical* is slang for "excellent" or "impressive" or "something that is true." Telling the truth wasn't something that came easy, especially when one of my first memories as a child was lying to a police officer. This was contrasted by my family, who were devoutly Catholic and often talked about the importance of honesty, integrity, and hard work.

My entire life was a contradiction. It was no wonder that studying a practice like yoga made sense later. Yoga is the study of paradoxes. Contradicting ideas designed to understand different aspects of the same truth. They are aspects of a *greater* whole.

Childhood is complex. On the one hand, you can see that perhaps lying to an officer is a bad thing. Lying to an officer at the behest of your parents can seem worse. However, if I told you the reason for the lie was to help save someone's life, would that make it better? Does it justify teaching a child that omitting the truth is okay? A child doesn't have the tools for discernment of this magnitude because they lack experience. Lying made me feel like I was all alone, disconnected from everyone and everything. I knew lying was wrong, but I was told to do it anyway. This isn't a call for listing all your parents' mistakes; it isn't about judgment either. We all falter in some way, but that's part of our learning process. This is about identifying the foundational cracks in your own experience that have kept you from feeling deeply rooted and supported in your life. Truth-telling is the foundational support we need to be and to feel radically loved.

Even as a child, the truth feels different from a lie. Can you think of a time in your life when you told your first lie? What was that like for you? It's confusing to be told one thing and feel another. Perhaps the fracture to our own self-trust begins here.

I became a disgruntled and troubled kid. I felt disconnected, hopeless, and often crippled by fear. I felt small, unseen, and insignificant. As I stood in that courtroom, I held on to an idea that I knew to be true in some deep and fundamental way—that maybe the support I needed was beyond what little knowledge I had.

My home was small and overcrowded. This made me seek out open spaces, and whenever I found them, I would feel a deep sense of relief. Maybe because I felt so much internal clutter. Going outside, being in nature, was the only thing that ever made me feel like I mattered. I would think about how the same force that created this planet may have also created me. The palm trees that lined the streets, the rare green space in a city park, the ocean—all felt like there was something bigger at play.

Wavering Faith

We were raised Catholic, which meant obey the rules or go to hell. If you don't go to church, you'll suffer. If you are mean to your abuelita, you'll suffer. If you don't go to sleep when your parents tell you to, you'll suffer. If you don't eat all your tortillas, you'll suffer. Suffering is the cornerstone of life.

My mother and father were both raised in Mexico. They lived in different areas of East LA before landing in a two-bedroom housing project. It didn't take long before it was overrun by drug dealers, gangs, and low-level pimps. It was during what is now called the "decade of death," when LA's yearly homicide rate was one thousand. Our single-story apartment was shared among ten people: my parents, sister, cousins, aunt, uncles, and abuelita. We experienced tragedy after tragedy. People losing their lives over senseless crimes, turf wars, and drug abuse. I had a tenuous relationship with God because of it. The reason why religion didn't make sense to me, despite the best efforts of my elders, is because of what I routinely saw in our neighborhood. Hell was something that existed *out there* if you were a sinner, not visibly on the streets of Los Angeles. Why would I try to be good if nobody else was abiding by the rules? I guess you could say I became spiritually bankrupt at a young age.

On a side note, I will use the terms "God" and "higher power" many times in this book. (I invite you to choose other words if you identify with a different source.)

As far as my parents were concerned, my sister and I were always being cared for. My abuelita saw to that. Roof over our heads—**check**. Food in our bellies—**check**. In some parts of the world, that's a feat in itself. Encouraging emotional stability, stress management, and making sure we felt safe wasn't part of their "how to raise a family" agenda. You can't transmit what you don't know. How are you supposed to teach something you've never been taught?

My abuelita hosted weekly rosarios (prayer circles) where all the neighborhood matriarchs would gather and pray for their families. The women would bring pan dulce (Mexican sweet breads) and hot chocolate. Although rosarios were the highlight of my week, they weren't always joyous. Increasingly, the women would ask for God's help, in tears for their children, some already in the throes of gangs or drugs.

I saw that my abuelita's faith never wavered, no matter how tragic events unfolded around her. Her morning ritual began at the crack of dawn. Her morning started in the kitchen to cook our meals for the day. Midmorning, she prayed before her altar in front of Jesus, the Virgin Mary, and a magazine tear-out of President Reagan. Her fingers moved through each rosary bead as she recited the Hail Mary and Our Father.

This was when I began questioning my faith. I asked her if she thought that God loved me.

She would reply, "Claro que si, mi amor" (Of course he does, my love).

I asked, "If God is so great, why did so many bad things happen? Why is he punishing all of your friends?" I quickly got scolded and was told that asking questions would make Jesus mad. Got it, questions equal wavering faith.

The final crack in my foundation came during my catechism incident. I was preparing for my First Communion. At a certain point during Sunday Mass, we headed to a nearby classroom to begin our lecture. Our teacher was a nun who I'm pretty sure hated children. On this particular day, the lecture was on the Eucharist, the wafer and the glass of wine. You confess your sins, take the take the wafer as a representation of God, sip the vino, and all your sins are forgiven.

The nun began the lecture, and I knew this was going to be off the hook. "Okay, children, when the priest raises the body of Christ at the time of the Eucharist, watch as God's hand comes in and touches it."

We filed back from our lesson to the church pews and our respective parents. We arrived as everyone inside the church was on their feet reciting the Our Father prayer. Expectantly, we fixed our eyes on the altar. As the priest raised the sacred wafer and recited, "Behold the Body of Christ," I looked at my friends as they all intently lasered into the empty space above the priest's head. I looked at my mother who was watching the priest and at my father who was half-asleep.

Wow, not one person realized that they were about to experience a freaking miracle right here at St. Anthony's church! I squinted my eyes so I wouldn't miss one single second. I saw nothing. Just empty space. I sat in silence and with a surge of anxiety as the sermon continued.

Our second meeting with the nun was called once parishioners filed in line and all the children made their way back to the lecture room. The nun was filled with joy. "Did you see it? Did you see God's hand come down and touch the Eucharist? Raise your hand!"

Everyone but me raised their hand.

"Rosie?" she said in a sardonic tone. "You didn't see God's hand come down and touch the body and blood of Christ?" she prompted.

"No, miss, I didn't. I didn't see anything."

"Oh, honey, don't worry, that means that you're not ready to take God into your life yet. Don't worry, it will come."

I had never felt like more of a failure in my entire life, but the nun's explanation just didn't sit well with me. If she had said it was more of a metaphorical "seeing," I would have had a different reaction. But when everyone in class described what they saw, there was no way I could say I saw something that I truly didn't. The realization of my damnation set in. *I.AM.GOING.TO.HELL.* Even after having lied to one of the highest forms of authority, I had to draw the line somewhere. It didn't feel right to lie in the House of God. I was terrified of going to hell. In that moment, I thought if I told the truth, maybe I would be forgiven.

My body jolted from my seat and in a low assertive voice I said, "Excuse me, miss. I didn't see anything, because there was nothing there!" I don't remember precisely what she said, but it went something along the lines of "Some kids are just destined to be without God." I was then asked to leave and not return until my attitude changed. I never did return, but it did change my attitude. Speaking your truth gets you *excommunicado*, got it. I went from obeying the rules to breaking them.

Getting Grounded

As I said in the introduction, you might not be where you *want* to be or where you *think* you should be, but you are in this moment in time nonetheless. To the best of your ability, you are safe, secure in your environment, reading this book. When you don't have your basic needs met, however, it is difficult to embark on spiritual pursuits, not because you can't but because your mind will focus on your basic need to feel safe and secure. All the tools we need to embark on our journey together are already here. You are radically supported. If you can pinpoint those moments in your life that inserted something within your mind that has not served you, it's time to reframe. The saying "If it's hysterical, it's historical," means that if a big emotion is triggered within you, there is probably historical data at its root. I didn't just end up in court because of one bad decision. There were several. As much as I could argue that I was a product of my environment, I still needed to take responsibility for the choices I made, and I needed to know that I would be supported to make a change.

For some, visualizing a life other than what they've experienced is very difficult. I know it was for me. We are all different, we have different needs, but at our core we all want to feel supported, loved, and connected.

Perspective

My abuelita planted roses in a tiny makeshift garden in front of our apartment. I loved watching her tend to her flowers and herbs; every morning before school she would water and talk to them. One day, as she prepared me for school, we walked out the front door to find her roses, herbs, and plants scattered on the ground, completely destroyed. I braced for her sadness as she held my hand. She bent down and picked up a handful of dirt and in Spanish said, "Look! They left the seeds! They will grow again." She carried on, sweeping the dirt as we made our way down the corridor. When I came home, she had replanted. As she fixed my dinner that same night, I sat on the counter and listened to her agitation: "The people who did this have no respect, which means they have no respect for themselves, they make idiotic choices, and they will never amount to anything. Plants are like people, they can be torn apart, but they will always grow back." I didn't understand why she wouldn't go searching for the people who did this. I assume it had to do with our safety. Again, as a child, it's difficult to discern because the world is complicated. I learned two things here: one, if someone upsets you, say nothing, and two, no matter how *sh*t* a situation is, it will at some point get better.

> They tried to bury us. They didn't know we were seeds.
>
> —MEXICAN PROVERB

Before we come back to what happened at my sentencing, here is what I had learned so far. We become marred by the battlefield of life, but we can use it to our advantage. It's easy to stay comfortable and accept the same stream of life; it's the turbulent current of change that creates the level of self-confidence we need in order to navigate the ever-changing landscape of life. We are built to withstand life's challenges.

Maybe you have seen the ugliest parts of life, and that's why you are here. Maybe you've never experienced the feeling of security and support that you've needed in order to heal. If you've experienced failure, loss, letdown, and the like, then you already have the discernment you need to move forward.

It's scary to look back sometimes, but you can either get swept away by the current of fear and disappointment or you can use it as a drive to take you to the places you've not ventured yet. If you feel like you've been stuck in the same place, in the same fish tank, maybe it's time to get that salt in your hair as the sun sets.

I AM RADICALLY SUPPORTED NOW

Here are some chapter takeaways to help you feel your own radical support.

1. **You must support yourself:** Take a deep breath; you got yourself here. You are both a river and a mountain. Rest in the truth.
2. See it, be it, feel it.
3. Inquire within.
4. Change your environment.
5. Affirmation: *Sometimes the only anchor you have is your own words, and the truth that you are right here, right now. Throughout your day, repeat the affirmation "I am radically supported."*

Questions for Journaling and Reflection

1. How did where you come from shape who you are?
2. What situation demonstrated that you are capable of change?
3. What does it mean to be radically supported?
4. How can you radically support others?
5. What is your definition of radical love?

Experience Exercise

One of the ways I like to find my roots is to literally connect to the ground. It's called *earthing* or *grounding*. Go outside and find a patch of grass or dirt. Spend anywhere from five to ten minutes focusing on your breath and feeling the connection of your body with the earth.

Earthing refers to contact with the earth's surface by walking barefoot outside. Creating a connection to the earth, or *grounding*, has most recently been used as a therapeutic technique that involves doing activities that "ground" or electrically reconnect you to the earth. According to the US National Library of Medicine, grounding is believed to be beneficial for inflammation, cardiovascular disease, muscle damage, chronic pain, and overall mood.

Contemplation: Grounding for Presence

* Get comfortable on the ground or in a chair.
* As you breathe gently, relaxing your shoulders, listen to the sounds of nature. Can you hear wind

blowing, birds chirping, cars driving by, or the
sounds of a city? Whatever is there, just listen intently as your body continues to relax.

* Bring to mind something from your past that has
helped shape who you are. Try to hold the experience without creating tension in your body.

* If there's tension, relax and breathe comfortably.

* As you breathe in, know that you are exactly
where you need to be, in this present moment.

* As you exhale, let go of the tension.

* Think of something/someone you are grateful for
and sit in gratitude and relaxation for a few
moments.

CHAPTER 2

YOU ARE RADICALLY CREATIVE

Radical Truth: Don't worry about
what everyone else is doing.

Los Angeles has been, and will always be, one big contradiction. It is the perfect expression of impermanence and the ever-changing qualities of creativity. It's rough, transient, and routinely demolished . . . but that gives the city character. It is also one of the most creative places on earth. There is a very distinct energy that LA possesses. For some, the invitation for creative expression exists every day. For others, it is a futile effort for survival. One of my favorite things about LA is that it is full of dreamers from all over the world. They come to the city glowing with potential, unapologetically unique and full of promise. That can be inspiring for some and intimidating for others.

Our environment shapes us, it gives us character.

The word *character* comes from the Greek *kharakter*, which means "engraved mark," or "to scrape or scratch." I am drawn to flaws because they make something unique. We are told that hardships build character, and I think creativity does as well. You must think creatively to move yourself out of hardship. Building character really means getting to know yourself at a deeper level. Experience + uniqueness + creativity = character.

Your experience makes you unique. It embeds a certain "secret sauce" in you that only you have access to. Your hopes and dreams have all been imprinted within you from a young age. Your secret sauce is that thing you do that is unique to you. It's the way that you problem solve, the way you can create something beautiful out of a not-so-beautiful situation. It's the way you inhabit the space you're in, the way you take up space. It's the way people are drawn to you. Only you. It's your ability to go with the flow, to be open to something new.

Quite often, we forget that our secret sauce is there because we might not think it's noteworthy, but at a deep level, you know it is. Your secret sauce is the reason you take certain chances. It's the reason you've made specific choices and the reason you want something more out of life. It's your essence and the way to access it is through experience and creativity. You must be willing to be open and honest

The grit of your experience keeps you honest.

with yourself though, and to tell the truth. The grit of your experience keeps you honest. That's where authenticity comes from.

Building Character

I was sitting on the bench at the courthouse, waiting for my name to be called. The desire to crawl out of my skin was unbearable. I listed and relisted all the ways I had disappointed my parents. I gazed at my mother in the distance, who was having a conversation with my public defender. She hadn't spoken to me in weeks. My family never had conversations about the future. Every week that passed was just one more to prepare them for the next. The way I escaped the guilt I felt was to not feel it.

Numbing was the key to surviving another day. Mindless activities like getting high made the time pass quickly and gave me friends to hang out with. Indulging in substances came to a screeching halt though when I almost died.

After my catechism incident, I developed a disdain for authority. I didn't know what to believe anymore. I wasn't interested in what anyone had to say. My mother dreaded any conversation with me because it quickly turned into a war of words. I left the house every day wearing my all-black uniform, which she hated. I wore all black for two reasons. First, because I didn't want to get caught wearing the wrong color in the wrong neighborhood.

Second, because black clothes felt like my mood. It was the perfect fashion statement for "I don't give a shi*t about what anyone has to say." I thought it was original, but I looked like every other teenager who shopped at Hot Topic. We will go to extremes to look and feel unique in an effort to be the same.

One day, when I got to school, my friends informed me that we were going to attend a "drug party." A guy picked us up in a beat-up Cadillac, and we drove around downtown for a bit. It was obvious the car wasn't his. We went down by Prospect Park, which is a small teardrop-shaped greenspace. Sometimes, we drove around this park in circles, for no reason. Eventually, we arrived at the apartment where the drug party was being hosted. As we approached the building, an older Hispanic gentleman walked by. He had a cane and was dressed in a Mr. Rogers sweater and had jailhouse tattoos on his hands. One of the boys I was with began tagging the side of the building.

The old man yelled, "You kids have no respect! You should respect other people's property and respect yourselves!"

I turned and walked away as fast as I could. A flash went through my mind of my abuelita cleaning up her dead plants. I still went to the party, though. I was thirteen years old, one of only two girls in the room, taking whatever paraphernalia the adult men handed me. I didn't know the weed they were smoking was laced with PCP.

I was unconscious when I arrived at the emergency room,

but soon the police showed up asking questions. I didn't answer any of them truthfully. We all lived in the same neighborhood after all. Nothing was said. The ramifications of this party left me with random but chronic and debilitating panic attacks. Instead of serving as a wake-up call, however, this emergency plunged me deeper into a state of fear.

As a child I was unapologetically vocal and confident, but as a teen, I became insecure, unable to control my emotions, and I was unable to speak up. Experience told me to shun my uniqueness and try to be like everybody else. I didn't fit any common molds. I didn't fit the mold of an addict, though I modeled addict-like behavior. That was my self-assessed diagnosis. I was familiar with the world of addiction through Alcoholics Anonymous. Several family members had experienced bouts of court-mandated sobriety, and I attended AA meetings with them. When people rose to the podium, they shared their stories. Some were honest; some, clearly not.

The truth just sounds different, doesn't it? It was unfortunate that after these meetings, my family members would come home with a newfound determination to get sober only to be seduced by our small, enabling tribe.

It was reported to my school that I had been hospitalized and needed "special attention." Basically, that meant since they didn't know what I would do, I needed to be monitored. For the rest of the school year, I had to spend lunchtime in the school library, aka detention. My friend Tommy was my library deten-tion buddy, and we talked a lot about death and dying. He was Filipino and his parents were practicing Buddhists. Tommy told me that Buddhists believe in the cycle of death and rebirth called samsara. He thought his brother, who'd been killed in a drive-by shooting, had come back as his pet iguana.

Buddhists believe they can change their lives through good karma to escape samsara, achieve nirvana, and end suffering. He picked up a book someone had left on the table, walked toward the front desk, put it in the "go back" bin, and said, "See? Good karma." I understood the basic principle of karma as similar to *do unto others as you would want them to do unto you.*

I asked him, "What if you keep doing good things and bad things still happen?"

"You just have to keep doing it," he said.

I thought that was too much work for zero payoff. Clearly he didn't understand that we are a reward-based society, and I am a reward-based doer. Good karma didn't sound like it was for me.

The Potential

We were called back into court after recess, and the judge began to read my sentence. He asked what had happened, and my pub-lic defender told me to explain everything. The flashback in my mind put me where I'd been that day, in front of Sierra Vista Park, where I relived my arrest.

I was walking home from school with my ditch buddy, about two blocks from our high school. We saw all the usual suspects—the other avid ditchers, the tagger crew, and some small-time drug dealers—at the park. We called ourselves "the rejects." The small grassy park had a basketball court and a primary-colored playground. As we walked up, we spotted two abandoned vehicles parked in front, doors wide open, engines still running—a red Honda Prelude and a black-and-white police car.

We got to the benches where everyone gathered, and someone said, "Aye, these five-Os just took off on foot after the guy who was driving the red Honda."

Wearing fingerless panda-print gloves, I pulled my black hoodie off my head, and one of the guys said to me, "You should go for a test drive."

I was already walking to the vehicles when someone else yelled, "ROSIE! Get in the cop car!" I thought that sounded like good advice, and I hopped right into the front seat, unaware that the park was crawling with undercover cops. A couple of seconds later, I looked in the rearview mirror and saw three more police cars closing in. I jumped out of the car and was surrounded by six officers, guns drawn.

"HANDS UP! GET ON THE GROUND! HANDS WHERE I CAN SEE THEM!"

They handcuffed me and took me to jail, where they ran my background check and saw that I'd had a few other minor run-ins with the local PD. The booking officer looked at me with a sly smile and said, *"Welcome to life in the system."*

Any chance of living a good life was disappearing before me. My public defender began to make a plea to the judge. She said, "Your Honor, I assure you that this young lady has potential. She has been influenced by her surroundings, but I know she doesn't deserve to go to jail."

The judge looked at me and read my verdict. "Probation for six months to one year. Depending on the defendant's progress, we will reconvene in six months."

This was a miracle. Every single person in the courtroom was surprised, including me.

This sentence was critical, and I needed to think long and hard about what I wanted to do to change my life. So, the next day, I ditched school and went to my favorite place to think.

Creativity Comes in Waves

I took the city bus to Venice Beach. I listened to music and looked out the window onto Sunset Boulevard, past the line of palm trees. The bus route ran through Beverly Hills, with its lavish mansions and expansive green landscapes, manicured lawns, manicured streets, and manicured people. It was idyllic and organized.

When I got to the beach, I kicked off my Dr. Martens and fidgeted with my Walkman. Venice has always been gritty. I walked past the head shops and beach squatters lounging in the sun. I found a spot near the shore and sat down, away from people but close to the waves that gently bubbled up to my toes before they made their way back to sea. I stared into the ocean, looking toward the horizon. My Walkman batteries died, so I was left with my thoughts and just enough spare change to get home.

A woman in the distance was walking along the water, holding her shoes in one hand and pulling up her pants with the other. Her shirt read, "Best Grandma on the Planet," with balloon letters and a big cartoon planet. She got closer and greeted me with a genuine smile. She stopped, and we chatted for a bit. She had a Midwest accent that sounded like Kitty Forman from *That '70s Show*.

"Shouldn't you be in school?" she asked, and I told her the truth.

There was something about her warmth and kindness that made me comfortable, plus the fact that I would probably never see her again. I told her I had ditched because I was in a bad situation and needed to figure out how to get better.

She smiled. "Well, I bet there's no problem that's bigger than that ocean, so you came to the right place." She continued talking about how we make situations in our minds bigger than they are, that's why she loved her community garden. She added that if we are overwhelmed, we need to stop and be kind to ourselves. If we do this, we will be more encouraged to tackle obstacles head-on, and that we need to learn from our elders and our community.

I wondered if she would feel the same way if I told her I had just tried to steal a cop car.

She said, "This is life, and whatever the situation, it will build character. You can always turn it over to God."

I wasn't going to ruin her last statement by telling her that "God's hand" never made it down to touch the wafer. What I understood from this grandma was that there is no situation that is as big as the massive body of water before us. Community gardens thrive with kind attention. That made sense. The waves went from being gentle and soft to a hard tumble that submerged my legs. Waves are always changing, always adapting to the tide. Each wave is unique, like us.

> Character—the willingness to accept
> responsibility for one's own life—is the source
> from which self-respect springs. Self-respect is
> something that our grandparents, whether or not

they had it, knew all about. They had instilled in
them, young, a certain discipline, the sense that
one lives by doing things one does not
particularly want to do, by putting fears and
doubts to one side, by weighing immediate
comforts against the possibility of larger, even
intangible, comforts.

—JOAN DIDION

I AM RADICALLY CREATIVE NOW

Here are some chapter takeaways to help you feel your own radical creativity.

1. **You must support yourself:** Take a moment to expand your vision. Instead of focusing in on something and creating tension, let your peripheral vision expand and relax. Go with the flow.
2. You are one of a kind.
3. Help comes in the most mysterious ways.
4. Nature is your teacher.
5. Affirmation: *Even when you don't feel like there is a way out of a situation, you must trust that*

change is possible. Throughout your day, repeat the affirmation "I am radically creative, and I honor and respect myself."

Questions for Journaling and Reflection

Putting it into practice: This really applies to anything in your life. Everything we do and think is a practice. We practice because we forget. It can be a hobby, a career path, a belief system, a childhood experience. What was the last thing you practiced for a long period of time without interruption?

1. What is your favorite characteristic (in yourself or in someone else)?
2. What experience taught you about your own resilience?
3. What is your "secret sauce"? (If you have a hard time answering this for yourself, employ two to three friends to either write it down or send you a voice note. It's best to hear it out loud.)
4. What experience in your life made you feel the most connected to yourself?
5. How do these experiences enrich your life?

Contemplation: Entering into Confidence

* Center yourself; if it's comfortable, close your eyes and breathe evenly.
* Bring to mind the last big decision you had to make and feel the confidence that was present when you made that decision.
* Imagine being without doubt and let your body relax and sink into the feeling of being in the fluid state of that confidence.
* Notice what it felt like in your body to just let the flow of confidence in.
* If any doubt arises, just exhale and return back to your breath and relax your body.
* Feel the excitement of making important decisions in your life from a state of confidence and peace.

CHAPTER 3

YOU ARE RADICALLY POWERFUL

Radical Truth: We like straight lines
because we can see what's ahead of us.
The unknown can be scary.

*Mindfulness: a mental state achieved by focusing
one's awareness on the present moment, while
calmly acknowledging and accepting one's feelings,
thoughts, and bodily sensations.*

Sometimes, you have to break something down before you
can rebuild it. Breaking down was aggressive and jarring for
me, but it doesn't always have to be that abrupt. We can begin
examining our lives by recognizing our obstacles. We can find
ways to gain clarity and then practice letting go. I didn't say,
"LET GO," I said, "Practice letting go."

My life had taught me that chaos was an opportunity to create something new. I had to believe I was creative enough to make necessary changes. When you become aware of what you are doing, and what is keeping you stuck in the same cycle, you have an opportunity to change. Simply by being aware of it.

Awareness is the key agent for **making change happen now**. Many yogic teachings focus on this very simple yet elusive fact. The mind and awareness are two separate things. When you are thinking, your mind is creating thoughts. When you are *aware*, you focus by observing your senses of sight, touch, taste, smell, and sound. Engaging all of our senses allows you to perceive more clearly and make better choices.

I learned growing up that being good meant you obeyed the rules and didn't make waves. Being bad meant that you broke the rules and made life chaotic. I had way more experience at being bad than being good. Being bad was *easy*. Being good was *hard*. I had to believe I was powerful enough to change my belief that I was never going to amount to anything.

After my court experience, everything felt different and I wanted to be different. A saying I'd heard during an AA visit repeated itself in my mind: "You can't go to the problem to find the solution." I wanted to be free from anxiety and fear, and I wanted to stop worrying about what everyone else was doing.

"You can't go to the problem to find the solution."

Practice

I was semi-ready to make small changes. My older sister had recently moved out of the apartment we shared with my mother and into the dorms at UCLA on the west side. She'd made it. She visited on the weekends and was the first person who told me about yoga. She did her stretches, and even though I made fun of her, she was—and still is—my hero.

My mom came home from work one day and left me a booklet with a note that read, "This might help your anxiety." The booklet was sticky and smelled like my baby sister's formula. It was called *Journey to Self-Realization* by Paramahansa Yogananda, an Indian yogi and guru who introduced millions of Indians and Westerners to meditation and yoga in the 1920s and '30s. The booklet was a collection of discussions about the path and purpose of life with guidelines to help meditators find genuine spiritual health and well-being.

I'd been without a spiritual practice ever since I'd been banished from catechism class. I was apprehensive about the booklet, but I was intrigued enough to take the bus to Hollywood to the closest Self-Realization Fellowship center. When I arrived, I was greeted with warm smiles, and a welcoming guide pointed me to the main building. It reminded me of the Taj Mahal, which I'd seen in my world history textbook. The scent of lavender emanated, and the air was thick with the smoke of something sacred. I sat on one of the pews, and an English-woman took the stage and began a short meditation.

As she spoke, I became distracted and scanned the room looking for *the guy* who would give the actual lecture. After a few minutes, I realized, "This lady is *the guy*." She was talking about how we are not only responsible for our own happiness but we also have the power to change and to live a life with purpose. She said we must "let go" of what isn't serving our highest good. I had never felt like I had any power, and now this stranger was telling me that I have power and I can change?

This was the first time I had listened to something that felt good and true that didn't involve hell, especially given the fact that I believed we were already in it. She said that prayer was *us* talking to *God*, and meditation was *us* listening. For us to access that power, we must be still and listen.

There was a fluidity to what I felt that day. The entire experience felt like it was not by chance. You know those moments? When everything feels perfectly coordinated and real. Some may call this a spiritual awakening.

It feels like a flowing river between your fingertips, or a calm breeze against your skin. This moment changed something; I went from hearing to listening. When you hear something, it is effortless and, at times, involuntary. When you are listening, you are focused and intentional. Meditation is a practice that must be, well, practiced.

Meditation gives you vitality and clarity. It provides a deep sense of calm so that you can sort through the mind's disarray. Meditation is something that you do, as well as something that you are. It's a direct connection to our higher power.

Spiritual awakenings do not have to be dramatic. They don't have to involve seeing visions, being visited by elite spirit beings, or feeling ecstatic. Your experience of connecting to something bigger can feel as simple as taking a spontaneous deep breath.

Letting Go

Beginning my meditation practice was challenging. I didn't know what I was doing, and I was afraid it wasn't a place I should venture alone. Closing my eyes reminded me of the dark alleys on my way home. If you ventured out on your own, you'd better be prepared. Always carry something that can double as a weapon or travel with a friend. I guessed that bringing a weapon to sit in meditation would be frowned upon. I had access to a few meditation tapes, and I purchased books at Barnes

& Noble. One book, *Wherever You Go, There You Are* by Jon Kabat-Zinn, was my first introduction to mindfulness. It took me five years to read the whole book, but I learned early on that if someone takes something from you, don't let them take your mind too.

The first time I meditated was a disaster. I sat on the apartment floor and closed my eyes. I didn't like that, so I tried staring at the carpet, seeing as much detail as I could. Most of it was pretty gross—crumbs, stains, mold, and all sorts of unpleasant smells from whoever had abused it before we lived there. It was not a relaxing experience, but I continued. Next, I tried closing my eyes for a minute or two at a time. Soon I realized that the more I *noticed*, the more at ease my body felt. I was no longer overwhelmed by the flaws in the carpet, or by the flaws of my own self. My mind wandered to memories of field trips to the Griffith Observatory and sweeping views of the brightly lit city grid that mirrored the constellations from the sky above. My body was calm and warm, like being wrapped in a blanket while enjoying a cup of Mexican hot chocolate. There were moments when I felt anxious, but my anxiety was quelled by my desire to just be in the present safe moment.

I'd love to end the story there and say that I became enlightened, started teaching yoga, and here we are today . . . but no.

Things changed slowly, I started to see things differently, and

I started taking classes at Santa Monica College. I was present in my life. I was practicing being myself. I was being mindful.

One day in class, my friend Carlos, whom I'd known since childhood, looked at me and said, "Rosie, you seem so different now. What happened?"

I didn't know how to respond. I wasn't sure if I'd just been insulted, so I pretended I had no idea what he was talking about.

He responded, "I know what it is!" He snapped his fingers and pointed at me. "You hit rock bottom! When people hit rock bottom, they either end up a lowlife or they turn into a success."

I took this in for a moment and wondered how the Dalai Lama would respond. I also wondered why my only options were being a lowlife or being a success. What if I just wanted to be different? I looked at him, shrugged, and said, "There is no rock bottom if you start from the bottom."

I was discovering what my own personal beliefs were and his comments made me realize that I while I believe in a lot of things, hitting rock bottom wasn't one of them. I have always thought that if you start from the bottom, it's all onward and upward from there. Sh*t rolls downhill, so if you start there, well . . . *anything* is better than sh*t, right? Rock bottom is giving up completely, it's lying down, wasting away, and letting yourself die. Rock bottom is living your life like a zombie, aimlessly going through the motions of existence, without senses, without color, without love. If you are alive, even after overcoming a difficult situation like a breakup, trauma, or job loss, you can rebuild. You can reactivate. You can reimagine. You have that power, and it is wise to start with small changes. If you are in a place that feels like rock bottom, I'm here to tell you, it's not. Rock bottom is the place where we begin.

What You Do Every Day

I worked a few mall jobs before I landed a position as a receptionist at a hair salon. I showed great leadership skills and was headhunted by celebrity hairstylist Jonathan Antin to manage his salon in West Hollywood. Part of my "secret sauce" was the ability to listen intently to what people needed. I could also remain calm when a customer was yelling or was extremely upset. I'd often think, *Damn, if this person was on the streets, they would not talk to anyone like this.* I just smiled and nodded. I became the salon's "calming presence," which was ironic. The girl who suffered from panic attacks was the one calming everyone down.

I loved learning how to run a business; experience is the greatest teacher. Jonathan had opened two salons as a self-made entrepreneur. His life as an entrepreneur and celebrity hairstylist was the basis for the reality television series *Blow Out* on Bravo. Jonathan taught me how to work with people, what to do and what not to do. He also taught me to not take sh*t from anyone, no matter what my background was. My past made me, but it didn't have to define my life. That salon is where I met my future husband.

Up to that point, my romantic relationships had not been great. I was still reeling from my beautifully checkered past and had experienced two long-term relationships. Both left me heart-broken, insecure, powerless, and overcautious. They were complicated, and I'd had enough of that during my childhood. I had sworn off men for good and my heart was closed for business, until I met Torry. I was working at the salon when a young, scruffy, artist-type guy walked up the front steps. He was kind, handsome, and polite. He exuded cool confidence that most likely had been there his entire life. He was a designer. It wasn't long before I began to call him "my future husband" (but not to his face). This is a lesson, don't ever close yourself off to love. It can arrive when you least expect it.

One Motörhead concert and a Mexican getaway later, I was planning the rest of our lives.

Finding the Flow

Everything that happens in your life is an opportunity to find new meaning; to let go of things that don't serve the highest vision of your life. If you can see it, you can be it. You can either look at compounding obstacles dog-piling on top of you or let things roll off your back and keep it moving. That's what letting go is. It's not ignoring or pushing away; it's the fluidity to let life move through you. The goal is to do it without attachment or expectation. Attachment is when you bond to something or some ideal. Expectation is when you have a deep belief, a confidence, that something is sure to happen. Expectation is premeditated resentment. Can you live a life without attaching to the results? Can you make decisions without having expectations? You can try. That's why it's called a practice.

Life is the biggest summit you are ever going to climb. Sometimes the only thing we know for sure is that there will be setbacks and we may have to go back and start over. The climb is treacherous, but it's your climb, unique to you. It belongs to you. You get to decide. Progress doesn't move in a straight line. There are dips and peaks; some plateaus as well, but there has to be steady and persistent movement. One foot in front of the other, chest up, shoulders back, keep your chin up, keep on keeping on, and that's what matters. Being present happens when you focus more on the journey than the destination.

Once I learned to be mindful about my life, to be present, I changed. I learned how to be part of a different kind of "system"; one that was readily avail-

Progress doesn't move in a straight line.

able and fully supportive of me making the best choices. I chose not to live in chaos but, instead, to thrive in creation. You have that same power.

What Is God?

The Universe, or as I like to call it, "God" in whatever form you believe, is an entity that is greater than us and that radically loves us all. When we can't see or feel that radical love, we need to step back, take responsibility for our choices, and show reverence to our circumstances, whatever they may be. Maybe we see it, feel it, or sense it. You are here, you are alive, and you are breathing. This is God.

I AM RADICALLY POWERFUL NOW

Here are some chapter takeaways to help you feel your own magnificent power.

1. **You must support yourself:** You become what you do every day; practice listening and trusting yourself. Empower yourself by acknowledging that you have the power to make your life better.
2. Let go of the possibility of failure.

3. Create moments for stillness.
4. Practice + let go + listen = change.
5. Affirmation: ***Taking charge of your life is the most powerful statement you make to the universe. Repeat the affirmation "I am radically powerful, confident, and strong."***

Questions for Journaling and Reflection

1. What is stopping you right now from being fully present in your life?
2. What resources do you need right now to help you get to the life you dream of?
3. Can you start today? Why or why not?
4. What would you want to create in your life if you could share it with the world?
5. Would you still do it if you knew no one would ever see it? Why or why not?

Contemplation: For Letting Go

* Find a comfortable space. Sit and rest your eyes.
* Begin to go through your day in your mind.

* Notice the first thing that came up; observe your body and your breath.
* Allow your breathing to be calm. Gentle inhale and slow exhale.
* How can you view this moment as something that will help create a deeper connection to your life?
* In your mind, move through your day once more, but this time choose a vantage point, a place where you can see from above.
* Notice if changing your vantage point creates a different perspective.
* Allow yourself to feel the charge of the things that felt uneasy today. Breathe in gently, then when you exhale, feel it melt away.
* Feel the peace of knowing that you've done your best today.

CHAPTER 4

YOU ARE RADICALLY PRESENT

Radical Truth: Inner work is not easy.
But unless you put in the effort, you won't
value what you've worked so hard for.

We make up to thirty-five thousand decisions per day. Thinking requires a lot of energy. The brain is only 2 percent of your body weight, but it uses 20 percent of your energy. That is wild. I became good at using most of that energy watching everyone live what outwardly looked like happy lives.

The first yoga book I read was *The Yoga Sutras of Patanjali* by Sri Swami Satchidananda. *The Yoga Sutras* is a highly regarded text that discusses the theory and practice of yoga.

I learned that one of the first things we must face when we arrive to our practice is our mind. It will do everything in its power to make practice difficult. The mind wants to be anywhere else but in the present moment. Right now, even as you read this, you are thinking about what you are going to do next, glancing at your phone, waiting for a notification, recalling something you need to do, or wondering where your delivery is. That's okay; it's totally normal.

Yoga begins now, in the **present** moment. Not the past, not the future, right now . . . and now . . . and now. Part of the mental discipline of yoga, meditation, and mindfulness is that we must do it consistently so that we build an **impression** in our mind. This impression compels us to do it daily. We create a habit.

According to yogic philosophy, these impressions are called samskaras. In Sanskrit, the word *samskara* is made up of the words *sam* ("joined" or "complete") and *kara* ("doing," "cause," "action"). When we do something over a long period of time, it ingrains our reactions, behaviors, and habits. One example we hear frequently is this: Samskaras are like sand mounds at the bottom of a lake. Above the surface you may not even know they are there, but they are.

These mounds represent our own conditioning. For example, if we drink alcohol daily, there will be an "I drink alcohol daily" mound. If you keep adding to the mound every day, it will build and grow until eventually you'll see a tiny mountain growing above the lake's surface. This will undoubtably disrupt the flow of water. These impressions aren't limited to habits, ideas, actions . . . almost everything can be part of your conditioning. Impressions can also be positive! For example, if you exercise daily, there will be an "I exercise every day" mound. However, it's the negative impressions that hinder our healing journey. Their repetition reinforces them and makes them difficult to resist. However, these can change over time. If you stop drinking alcohol every day, then you begin to take away from the "I drink alcohol daily" mound and begin to add to the "I didn't drink alcohol today" mound.

Samskaras are patterns and habits that generate the way we unconsciously react to the world at large depending on how deep or vast these impressions are.

When our impressions come to the surface, there are three ways we can choose to react: The first way is to avoid the experience altogether. In the second, we compound the impression by adding fuel and making it a more intense situation. In the third, we can try to become aware of it and do our best to remain objective and remain neutral.

You exhibit the same habits every day, most of which existed long before you embarked on this journey. When you decide to create a practice, like meditation, it simply serves as a stadium where you can become the spectator to all the deeply rooted impressions that exist in your mind.

Palm Trees and Dreams

When I was little, teachers would ask, "What do you want to be when you grow up?" I would give the standard answers—doctor, teacher, mermaid. In reality though, what I really wanted was to be a palm tree. I consider the palm tree to be the disco ball of the tree family. They are tall, slender-stemmed, and have pinnate leaves that create perfectly sharp edges. They are unapologetic about taking up space. On many family outings my uncle would sarcastically quip, "City of Angels, nothing but palm trees and dreams." Most think living in LA as like living in paradise, but make no mistake: there is wrought iron on the windows for a reason. Palm trees were as close to nature as we got. Any city dweller knows that living in a city is a different kind of wilderness.

Palm trees are also tall and skinny, which is everything society had conditioned me to believe was ideal. The more time I spent in the beauty industry, the more uncomfortable I became in my own skin. I had an "I'm not skinny enough" mound or impression. As a teenager, I thought I was overweight and unhealthy because I loved to eat homemade Mexican food and hot dogs from 7-Eleven. In Latin families, being a little gordito or gordita is not a terrible thing. It's not healthy, but it's not necessarily frowned upon. I didn't really care about my body. It was a shell that needed to do what I wanted it to do, when I wanted to do it. I didn't respect it.

I didn't have a great relationship with food, and oftentimes, I ate my feelings; I had been on anxiety medication for years, and when I stopped taking it with the approval of my doctor, I gained fifty pounds. In my early twenties I discovered that purging was a great way to control how much I ate. It was part of the toxic diet culture I was surrounded by. One of the stylists I worked with said that only "skinny girls" are successful. She showed me pictures of girls on magazine covers and said, "If they were fat, they wouldn't be on here." Then she made her way to the conference room and counted her french fries.

The LA Yoga Scene

I found a yoga studio close to where Torry and I lived. I was apprehensive to start because up until this point, I had only practiced yoga on my own, using books I checked out from the library. Your first day at any studio or fitness class is a lot like the first day of school. You have to be okay with being a little awkward and uncomfortable, not knowing where anything goes or where to stand. Depending on the type of person you are, you might show up and make friends instantly or you might decide to check the situation out a bit and wait until someone talks to you. Or you can ignore everyone to save yourself the trouble of having to make friends. I was the latter. It took a while for me to get over the feeling that yoga wasn't for me. I didn't wear the right clothes and I didn't want to commit to buying a mat or spending my hard-earned cash on yoga pants. Torry was supportive but would also occasionally poke fun and ask if I was bringing my cult robes in my backpack. I always left the house in my black hoodie and sweats.

My discomfort began as I entered the building. I prepared for it by placing my headphones on and avoiding eye contact. A sea of fancy yoga legs bustled up the stairs to the lobby. Some greeted each other with hugs as others perused the retail area. I overheard two women talking about how the studio needed to replace the mirror in the bathroom because it made them look "fat." I stood against the wall, only occasionally looking up to smile at a stranger.

A girl walked by with a shirt that read, "Yoga Gang." Yeah, okay? I guess they have gangs for everything these days. The front-desk gal with the half smile handed me my rental mat with the phone pressed to her ear. I made my way to the back of the room, which had an alternate exit door. Perfect. My oversize hoodie was big enough to cover the sides of my face, so I didn't have to interact with anyone once I found my space. My mind wandered, and I began to think about what it would be like to have yoga friends.

"Weird," I told myself. "They're probably weirdos."

I continued attending classes, but every time a class started, the impressions began playing in my mind: *You aren't flexible enough. You can't do any of these poses.* I was uncomfortable in my own skin and debated leaving class 85 percent of the time. If something felt too hard, I told myself, I could go home. If the teacher I liked wasn't there, I could go home. I would give myself incentives like, *If you finish, you can grab a bagel from the place downstairs*, or *If you finish, you can have pizza for dinner.* I thought about how often I made fun of my sister for extending her arms and bending her legs when she would practice yoga in the living room.

I heard teachers say things like, "Lean into the discomfort. Still the fluctuations of your mind and surrender," with long winded *eeeeeerr*s at the end. Surrender? Nothing chapped my butt more than this word. To me, surrender meant death. It meant giving up on life and giving way to the victimhood that plagued my childhood. I didn't get here by surrendering. I got here by pushing hard and crying on the inside, like a winner. I didn't allow myself to relate to anyone else because I didn't think anyone else would understand me. The discomfort and negativity I felt was relentless. I quit postures halfway through because I got angry that I couldn't achieve the level of dexterity and grace my neighbors had. Comparison is the greatest killjoy.

Comparison is the greatest killjoy.

Class always ended with the same final posture. Sweaty bodies settled onto their backs for Savasana, also known as corpse
pose. Savasana represents the final rest that integrates the entire
practice. The work is done, and now it is time to relax. My cue
to exit. I didn't need to rest before I started my day. I needed to
get to work! This continued year after year. I built an "I practice
yoga" impression (albeit sloppily) as I continued showing up and
doing my best at the studio. I took away from my "I can't practice yoga" impression, and it seemed like it was beginning to
create awareness to all the other impressions that had been a
lifetime in the making.

Sometimes I left class agitated, debating whether yoga was
serving me or if I was stuck in an abusive relationship with it.
Moments of stillness left me feeling more frenetic.

It had been a particularly difficult spring when I finally decided to stay for an entire class. The salon had been intensely
stressful. Torry was going through hard times in his business,
and the country was talking about an impending stock market
crash. The year was 2008.

I don't know how I got a spot in the overcrowded yoga studio. Toward the end of class, the teacher walked over to my area,
carefully scrolled through a playlist, and warmly looked at me
with a smile. She glanced over at the clock, looked back at me,
and motioned to the door with her eyes. She knew that I would
always leave around this time. I gracefully smiled back and

gently shook my head. *No. I'll stay.* Her surprised and enthusiastic smile was followed by a thumbs-up as she mouthed, *Okay.*

She disappeared and then reappeared with a blanket and a bolster. I moved away from my mat as she rolled the blanket like a burrito and placed it horizontally on the mat. She asked me to lie down with the blanket behind my legs, then placed the bolster vertically along my spine. She disappeared and then reappeared with another blanket and placed it behind my head like a pillow. "Lay back and just relax." She walked away, and I lay there uncomfortably, still trying to keep my body rigid. I looked around and began to see everyone close their eyes and float into bliss.

I could feel my breath deepening as I listened to the sounds of Tibetan bowls in the distance. I thought of the moment when I was a child and heard my first drive-by shooting, watching my belly rise and fall. I felt my body contracting again.

"Just breathe," I told myself. "You're okay." I let my arms release, felt my upper body soften. And felt like my entire body was moving deeper into the ground. I felt a trickle of water move down the side of my cheek, then another, then another. I opened my eyes as they welled up with saltwater. I could see a palm tree through the short and narrow window above the Buddha shrine. I let the tears stream down the side of my face.

Moments later, I emerged and made my way to my car feeling a deep sadness. Time was passing. My life was a current, a quick-flowing river. I was a spectator, idly watching as the stream flowed to different places, hurried, and without direction. I spent so much time worrying about what everyone else was doing that I hadn't stopped to think for myself. I had created unhealthy impressions. Although not all of them were negative, the ones I had let live in my mind needed to go.

The promise of yoga and meditation is to make the unconscious conscious. It's bringing to light the mounds that lie below the surface. When you experience moments that leave deep impressions, you don't need to dissect them. You don't need to figure out how or why they worked. They worked. That's enough to move forward.

The moments that shape your life—moments of trust, doubt, peace, uncertainty—they all lead you to wisdom, which, in turn, leads you to healing. You gain a deeper knowledge, to discern the journey to your own unique spiritual center. You are forged in the fire and shaped by your adversity. This journey is the path you need to take to become the person you are meant to be— unapologetically and radically *you*.

Growing Pains

Many of us get addicted to the stories we tell ourselves about *why* we aren't where we want to be. We tell ourselves that we don't care or that we really didn't want something, but we have created impressions in our minds that *The mind will* say otherwise. Maybe we weren't born *not stop, but it* into it. Maybe our bodies weren't meant *can be directed.* for it. Maybe we aren't enough. There's a fine line between recognizing shortcomings and setting up camp there.

Growth is uncomfortable. In order for you to grow, you must recognize what your impressions/patterns/habits are, especially if they weren't placed there by you. Remember, *you* get to decide whether to perpetuate patterns, impressions, and repeat habits. Repetition creates and reinforces new impressions.

Notice how these impressions affect your body, even right now. Observe if there is any tension, and relax your shoulders. Take a deep breath. The mind will not stop, but it can be directed. Allow your experiences to serve as catalysts to challenge unhealthy narratives, habits, and beliefs. The mind is powerful, and it is here to support you. If you want to change something, you have to recognize and take action differently. In order to rebuild, we must first break things down, remember? Negative patterns, habits, and beliefs can change. No one will do it for you. This is the ultimate act of self-care and self-respect. Discerning what *will* and *won't* serve your "highest good" is hard, but it is possible. You can attempt, again and again, to let go of attachments that cause you harm.

You are both fluid as a river and grounded as a mountain.

You are one of a kind. The love you seek is already here, present, in this moment, and this moment, and this one.

(K)NO(w) Surrender

I think the word *surrender* should be accompanied by "and." Surrender and do the work to feel more grounded, more connected. When you feel helpless, help someone. I believe that we must get to know surrender, like getting to know a friend. Surrendering can be an opportunity for a deeper connection to yourself, a deeper connection to (God, a higher power, ____). Connection is radical love. Surrendering with action creates opportunities for transformation. We don't experience love in the past or in the future, we experience it right here, right now. Surrender, and know.

I AM RADICALLY PRESENT NOW

Here are some chapter takeaways to help you feel present and ready to cocreate your own life.

1. **You must support yourself:** Acknowledge the impressions in your mind that aren't serving you.

Know and trust that you can slowly but surely minimize them by being present in your own life.

2. Make surrender your friend.
3. Positive impressions build quickly.
4. Repetition is the key.
5. Affirmation: *Direct your attention to what you want to feel and feel it now. Repeat the affirmation "I am radically present, right here right now."*

Questions for Journaling and Reflection

1. How often do you compare yourself to others?
2. What does surrender mean to you?
3. What was the most powerful decision you had to make in your life? How long did it take before you saw any results?
4. How often do you make time to think about your dreams?
5. If you could spend your time doing something you love without worrying about resources, what would it be? Why would you do it?

Contemplation: Relaxed Present Awareness

* Go outside and find a quiet space.
* Allow your attention to be consumed by the life that is happening around you.
* Listen to whatever sounds are present, and feel yourself immersed as if you were in an amphitheater.
* Bring your awareness to your breath, inhale, and exhale calmly and smoothly.
* Now, think of something that is weighing on you; as you do, have the intention to relax your body.
* As you breathe in, feel the weight subside, and as you exhale, feel it move out of your body and into the space before you.
* Bring yourself back to the sounds and the space around you.
* Repeat this as many times as you wish until you feel a deeper sense of comfort.

PART II

BODY

When the volume of negativity and fear
is turned up, our body can help us
move through it.

CHAPTER 5

YOU ARE RADICALLY RESPECTED

Radical Truth: You might be a diamond in
the rough, but remember, you're still
a diamond. Act accordingly.

Self-Respect

I respected other people more than I respected myself. My body, my money, and my time. Self-respect is essential for your confidence and happiness and for feeling radically loved.

When you lack self-respect, you value other people's opinions of you more than your own. You value everyone else's time more, and you overindulge in habits that don't serve you. Your environment is full of clutter, and you exhaust yourself trying to be all things to all people. You omit the truth for fear of making waves, and you lack the ability to see beyond the perimeter you've created.

When you have self-respect, you no longer feel the need to compare yourself to other people. You value your time and respect your body. You build yourself up by nourishing your mind, body, and spirit. You create an environment that is decluttered and with items that reflect your character and bring you joy. You remain honest and communicate how you feel. You speak your truth. You listen intently. You have healthy boundaries and respect your time. You honor your failures and see them as valuable to your growth. That is self-respect.

The only way I was able to see this was by recognizing how I just threw myself into everything I did. I let other people's lives infiltrate my own. I am a nurturing water sign, so I have a disposition to give up all of myself to caretake someone else's needs. This is not sustainable. At some point, these cracks will turn into fractures that are difficult to mend. For some, it may show up later in life in the form of an abrupt job change, a breakdown, an affair, or an addiction.

I was working so much I hadn't had a chance to stick my toes in the sand. The salon didn't survive the housing crash. I got a job as a personal assistant working in Malibu, and I took solace in being able to see the ocean. The ocean had always given me a sense of grounding and helped me remember *I am still here*. It had been months since I had done that.

Torry and I were having a particularly difficult time in our relationship, which I decided to ignore, and instead I put all my energy into my career. In college, I changed my major several times, and I frustrated Torry with my ever-changing career ideas. If it sounded interesting, I wanted to try it on for size. The more I practiced yoga, and the more I meditated, the more I realized how unhappy I was. I was experiencing withdrawals from my anxiety medication, and my body was starting to feel it. I woke up with back pain, everything I ate was bland, my joints were inflamed, and my head hurt constantly.

Self-Esteem

Typically, if you feel well, you don't go into the world of wellness. You go into this space because at one point or another, you felt unwell. I felt low in every area of my life, and this became magnified by my newly active life on social media. I believed I would find relief, not inside my body but somewhere "out there." I realized I had an issue with my body when I looked in the mirror one day and the first reaction was, "Ugh, I need to do more cardio."

On the outside, I looked healthy, but I was far from it. Everyone wanted to know what I was doing to get so "fit." I imagined telling them some elaborate and highly detailed healthy eating plan. Then I imagined telling them the truth, *On my breaks I just go to the bathroom and make myself throw up. Oh, and I do yoga.*

We turn to the health-and-wellness world to restore our health, yet its very structure reaffirms how inadequate we are. If we are too skinny or too fat, too big or too small, it means we are unhealthy. If we are too old, too young, have too much cellulite or too many wrinkles . . . fuhgeddaboudit. It would have been more beneficial had we learned about proper nourishment and self-respect when we were kids. To learn the true meaning of what health is for us. If the definition of *health* is to be free from illness and injury, can we be curvy and healthy at the same time? *The short answer is YES!*

Nourishment and health are about bio-individuality. It should be tailored to the individual. There are far too many of us to count who deprive ourselves to meet a superficial, unrealistic standard. One person's food can be another person's poison. The best approach for supporting your nutrition is to learn what works for *you*. When you respect your body, you want to treat it well, like a loving friend. Not like a garbage disposal or an enemy.

What we eat reflects our attitudes, thoughts, and overall well-being. We find ourselves, however, too busy to make home-cooked meals and we rely on convenience foods that we know aren't good for our health. Most people pay little attention to where their food comes from, how it's treated, or how it will affect their bodies when they consume it. Although the SLOW (sustainable, local, organic, and whole) foods and farm-to-table movements have increased awareness about organic and wholesome eating, we are largely a society that just wants to feel good. However, access to these healthier food options have yet to enter the mainstream in a way that is affordable to anyone below a upper-middle-class income level. In addition, the people that do have the means to afford a healthier food option often prioritize convenience over sustainability or health.

Studies show that many factors influence our feelings about food and our eating behaviors, including our culture, socioeconomic status, genetic background, and psychology. For example, I was taught that not finishing everything on my plate was disrespectful. We often visited family members and family friends who hosted gatherings and provided meals. None of them were in a financial position to feed a large group of people, but they did it anyway, out of love. So if we were offered something, it was rude not to eat it. The impression this left on me was that even if you are full, you must eat everything to the point of discomfort. One of the biggest issues that impacts self-esteem is the feeling of not having control. If that happens when you are young, it can be challenging to establish boundaries when you get older.

After I completed my first yoga teacher training. I delved deep into yoga philosophy. I consumed countless books and signed up for every workshop I could, oftentimes doing karma yogi work (yoga in action). In exchange for classes, I'd clean the studio. I learned about the different yoga schools, and about yoga's ancient Indian roots.

I was exploring yoga as a new career path. I wanted to know what the "secret sauce" was that made yoga so effective for me. I noticed that while I was in teacher training, I shifted my perspective more often. My teachers would say things like, "How you do anything on the mat is how you do everything in life." I was less reactive and becoming more patient. I noticed it the first time while driving on the 405 freeway. This freeway is God's design for testing patience. You don't actually drive on the 405. You move at a glacial pace. I noticed myself just in the zone, moving through the lanes, patiently waiting for people to pass, making space for people with more important places to be. I also noticed a difference in my ability to speak my truth.

True, Necessary, and Kind

When you can speak your truth, it's easier to feel empowered and supported. Speaking your truth can take many forms. It can be expressing your opinion or how you feel, or stating your own values. It can be telling the truth about how you feel or something that you are going through.

Most often, if we hold our truth back, it's because we are in fear that someone may think differently of us. They may get offended or triggered. The easiest way to speak your truth is to ask, "Is it true, is it necessary, is it kind?"*

Being unable to fully speak your truth causes the most suffering for one person—you. Find someone, or a group of people, who can listen to you. There should be at least one person in your life who you can be radically honest with.

I started going to AA meetings with my friend—whom we'll call O—who was addicted to cocaine. O had recently blown up their life and gotten fired from their job, so I recruited O to become my first yoga student. We had long conversations about life and what it would look like to help other people. I had learned that the key to feeling less helpless was to help someone else. I told O about the many people I knew who had achieved full recovery attending AA meetings. O was feeling good. They were in that euphoria that comes with being newly sober. My regular attendance at AA meetings helped me realize that I had a problem too. I'd thought I could stop purging at any time, but I never stopped long enough to see if that was true. What I learned alongside O was that my habit was dangerous and very

---

* This is a paraphrase from the Anguttara Nikaya V.198: "It is spoken at the right time. It is spoken in truth. It is spoken affectionately. It is spoken beneficially. It is spoken with a mind of good-will."

prevalent among women struggling with addiction. I had a deep *impression* that I needed to eradicate.

At one meeting, a beautiful, statuesque Amazonian goddess with dark brown hair approached the podium to speak and lead the meeting. She was supposed to be celebrating ten years of sobriety, but she relapsed when she went home to Texas for her father's funeral. Her mother had passed from complications with cancer the year before, and she described in detail how she couldn't think of a better opportunity to not feel anything. "I'm an orphan now," she said. "I always said I felt alone in the world, but I wasn't, I had them and they loved me. Now the only two people in the world who loved me are gone." She continued, "I drank everything I could, and then decided I needed to throw it up. As I was over the toilet sobbing, crying out for my mother, I made a choice. As much as it hurt, it was okay to start again from the beginning. So that's what I'm here to do."

O and I just looked at each other. Both of us had tears in our eyes. When the meeting concluded, O hugged her and told her she wasn't alone.

The three of us went to a local café for a bite. We talked about life, love, and loss. The three of us were from different backgrounds, we had different upbringings, grew up in different states, but we all understood one another. We listened intently as one person shared, then the other. We laughed, we cried, and not one of us noticed that we'd been at the café for four hours.

We were present, sharing love, feeling loved, speaking our truth. There was no unsolicited advice, no "should-ing" on one another. Just fully expressing and listening. After that meeting, O struggled for years, but after several failed attempts, they got and remained sober to this day. The Amazonian goddess is their sponsor.

Failing Forward

The first studio I attempted to teach at in West Hollywood said I needed to audition. This studio hosted all the locally known yoga teachers in LA, and I really wanted to teach there. The requirements, if you were lucky enough to be "invited to teach," were to be recommended by another teacher, to have lots of Instagram followers, and to teach the owner a twenty-minute class. Also, you needed to bring a headshot. *Why does what I look like matter?* To me, yoga is about the mind, body, and spirit connection. It's about connecting to your body and breath; a means to learn discernment and my connection to a higher power. It's about union. When I showed up to my audition, there was a giant mural on the wall that read, "Yoga for Everybody." The people in the class were two teachers who already taught at the studio, the studio manager, and three of their regular students.

I was getting ready to pull off my hoodie when the studio manager said, "You're gonna take that thing off, right? We need to see your body." I taught my class as best I could, focusing on alignment and anatomy. During one of my college career flips, I had taken a few premed anatomy classes. I quit soon after we began dissecting cats. When I completed the yoga class, I left feeling good.

After a week, I called the studio to check in. The studio manager struggled to remember *which one* I was before they said, "Oh, the girl wearing the hoodie," followed by "We're looking for someone who's fit, and you're not fit enough."

So much for "Yoga for Everybody."

This story is important for two reasons. First, it showed me that I needed to trust my gut. I knew the minute I walked in that this was not the place for me but I did it anyway. Second, it demonstrated that I had the strength to move past failing at something I **thought** I really wanted.

I mentioned this to my therapist at the time, who was helping me with my eating disorder. She said, "You are learning to 'fail forward' and learning how to set boundaries, and this is a good thing." It's important to respect our failures because they give us direct feedback. This was another way I was able to build self-respect, by not dwelling on the things that didn't work out. Not getting that teaching job taught me that what we *think* we want and what is *best* for us can sometimes be on opposing sides.

Listening

My assisting job took over my life, and I severely neglected my health and relationships. Any time you're hyperfocused on one single area of your life for too long, the other areas of life—your spirituality, hobbies, friendships, creativity, and homelife—suffer. Anything outside of work was effed. My body was giving me all the feedback I needed, but I wouldn't listen. I heard subtle internal worries, but I ignored them. I felt the same anxiety and depletion I once had as a teenager, except now it was worse. When you become aware and you practice how to feel good, your body will tell you when it doesn't. It's the elephant in the room, but instead of seeing it and acknowledging it, you try your best to wedge yourself around it, moving like it's not there.

My friend Andres was between acting jobs. He was taking some personal training classes and offered to train me in exchange for yoga classes. I started training slowly by walking on a treadmill while listening to music, because I didn't like to sweat. He suggested I try running. I hated running more than anything in the world. Running was what we did when we were trying to get away from cops. It was not considered a leisure or fitness activity. He felt it might be liberating for someone who was under stress. So if I was going to start running, I was going to do it right. I signed up for the LA Marathon. Sometimes when you aren't listening to yourself, you lose your self-trust. You make unsound decisions. I thought that if I could run 26.2 miles and survive, I could do anything. I wasn't thinking about the actual training and the stress it would put on my body.

Completing my first marathon was a huge feat. I wasn't concerned with my time but, rather, with finishing the race and not dying in the process. It was a way to take my focus off work and everything else that was going on in my life. I was replacing emotional stress with physical stress.

I'm a serial monogamist. The stress in my job and homelife were getting more intense and wearing on me. I woke up anxious, dreading the day, thinking, *What kind of fire are we putting out today?* I had outgrown it. I loved my boyfriend, but he was going through a major legal battle, and both our families needed our attention with standard issues that families go through. We were the glue that held our families together, and when something happened to one of them, it spilled over on us. Life was happening. The more intense the anxiety and stress, the farther I ran and the more I pushed my body. If you don't respect your body, you will push it until it shuts down on you. I was abusing my body to avoid layering other people's stress on top of my own. Emotion can't hit a moving target. I understood now why so many of my friends in recovery turn to numbing. I couldn't go down the path of substances myself, so I ran, as hard as I could.

Be Humble

When I finally quit my job, I got an earful. My friends and family didn't understand why I would leave the safety of a paycheck. I told them, "Because I wasn't happy, and it wasn't serving my ability to respect myself." A job without boundaries is a recipe for disaster. It's not sustainable. So many of us are willing to do things that don't make us happy. To be clear, it's not your employer's responsibility to make you happy. It's your job to make yourself happy. There should never be any job that is beneath you. It's imperative to respect every job, because every single job teaches you how to respect yourself and respect others.

Respecting yourself teaches everyone else how to respect YOU. Being humble is the key. Oftentimes people feel that being humble is about being submissive or acquiescing to the demands of others. That couldn't be further from the truth. There's a difference between being humble, putting your time in, and the need for approval. When I worked at the salon, an assistant couldn't become a stylist until they had put their time in. They needed to earn a stylist chair by doing the not-so-glamorous work—sweeping floors, serving coffee, organizing cabinets, running errands, and doing laundry. Nothing was given, everything was earned. Self-worth, self-confidence, and self-esteem are the direct results of taking your time to do what needs to be done to serve your highest good.

There's a Latin motto, *Palmam Qui Meruit Ferat*, which translates to "Let whoever earns the palm, bear it." Anything worth having requires effort. It requires tenacity. We must be persistent and purposeful so that we can become resilient. Tenacity is the salsa of everyday life. We need to be tenacious to learn to distinguish whether what we are doing is working. Whether or not it is worth our time. Anything worth having is worth working for, and this builds self-respect. If you want something to stand the test of time, it's going to take time.

Love Is a Battlefield

The Bhagavad Gita is a Hindu sacred text originally written in Sanskrit that forms part of a larger epic, the Mahabharata. Yoga is presented in the Bhagavad Gita as the process by which a person can connect with the absolute or divine.

The Bhagavad Gita is a narrative told through a dialogue between Arjuna, a warrior, and his charioteer, who is the god Vishnu disguised as Krishna. Arjuna doubts whether he should go into battle, and Krishna explains that he must fulfill his dharma, or duty, as a warrior. In his explanation, Krishna discusses various types of yoga, including Jnana, Bhakti, Karma, and Raja.

One of my yogi friends has an aversion to this text because of its inherent "nonspiritual" setting on a battlefield. She thinks it's important for us to evolve and make our own choices without the insertion of a third-party directive, like in this poem. I disagree. The story serves as a metaphor for our internal battle, the battle we are constantly fighting; the struggle of making choices. In our journey to healing and to mastering our own life, action is inevitable. It is the representation for life as we know it. The truest expression of love.

I AM RADICALLY RESPECTED NOW

Here are some chapter takeaways to help you feel more self-respect.

1. **You must support yourself:** Practice listening to what your internal dialogue is saying to you. Notice if your instinct is to ignore or talk yourself out of something that doesn't feel aligned. Can you give yourself the time and space you need to give way to the fullest expression of yourself?
2. Nourish yourself well.
3. Speak your truth, listen intently.
4. Do the work, be humble, and earn it.

5. Affirmation: *Your body gives you direct feedback, listen to what it says or does when you repeat this affirmation "I honor and respect my body, my mind, and my spirit."*

Moving Practice and Affirmation

Go for a walk, jog, spin, or run. While you are moving, repeat one or all of these affirmations:

* I am grateful for my body and my breath, and I am supported.
* Love is a vast ocean. I am a wave of change.
* My mind is strong, my body is healthy, and my heart is open.

Contemplation: Present and Breathing

* Sit comfortably, and take three clearing breaths.
* Tune into your body, observe any areas of tension, begin to relax.
* With your inhale, breathe in for four counts (1-2-3-4) and out for five counts (5-4-3-2-1). Do this a few times.

* Begin to bring to mind something in your life that you put a lot of effort into. What were the fruits of this work? Can you find the lesson?
* Continue to breathe smoothly and calmly, and imagine being in your body and everything feeling relaxed, calm, and confident.
* When you are ready, open your eyes and observe what is present for you, let whatever emotions come up to the surface. Move into your day, knowing that if you can see it, you can create it.

Mindful De-Stressing Techniques

* **Engage your senses.** Practice yoga, go for a walk, dance, sing karaoke, meditate, listen to your favorite album from start to finish. Try to engage all of your senses so that you feel fully present.
* **Find your friends.** Send your best buds a voice note. Listening to someone's voice that you love releases oxytocin (the feel-good hormone). Be mindful, send something heartfelt, and end with a question so that they know you want to hear from them.
* **Moments of stillness.** Boredom is a symptom of not paying attention. Instead of reaching for your

phone when you are bored, be still, in silence. Be bored. Sit outside, or on a chair or couch. Pay attention to what is present; moments of stillness are perfect moments for connecting to your higher power.

CHAPTER 6

YOU ARE RADICALLY RESILIENT

Radical Truth: Never is always wrong.
Always is never right.

What does it take to be happy? Some ask this too many times, some not enough, but the answer is usually the same. "I'm not doing enough" or "I'm doing too much," and I'm not happy. We have all sorts of impressions, beliefs, and ideals that we think will make us happy. Some include success, money, traveling, romantic relationships, friends, and so on. Remember what I said in chapter 4 about impressions? What happens if you continue to feed one belief? It builds until at some point it shows itself to the world. Your priorities are all around you. They are the choices you make every day. They are who you choose to spend your time with, what you spend your money on, what you eat, even what you choose to think. We make choices based on what we think will bring more happiness. For some, these choices may rest in avoiding difficult situations, conflict, or speaking their truth.

Finding happiness does not rely on something that is external. The key to finding happiness rests in your resilience. It rests in your ability to face your fears, learn new things, and recognize your unique strengths. Resilience is your ability to bend, not break. We were built to withstand storms for a reason. When you have a paper cut, your body has everything it needs to heal itself. You don't need to order a "heal paper cut kit" online. Your body knows what to do, and it just does its thing. You've been on the planet long enough to know that if you don't bend on your own, life will do it for you.

I had a hard time finding and cultivating happiness. Even though I read every self-help book I could find, and purchased spiritual commodities, happiness always eluded me. I rarely gave myself the opportunity to slow down. In fact, I decided to train for another marathon, just to avoid being still. I believed that momentum equaled success and success ultimately led to happiness. Therefore, the more I moved, the less I felt and the less likely I was to realize that my life was falling apart. Emotion can't hit a moving target.

Unemployed, struggling with my relationship and self-worth, I decided to put all my focus, once again, on running. All of the mindfulness techniques I'd learned sat in my closet, along with my dusty meditation cushion. I'd learned the importance of paying attention but refused to see that I was avoiding everything. I was struggling with self-doubt. The internal chatter of *Did I make a mistake? Should I have quit my job?* Grocery shopping was a gamble to see if my debit card would get declined. My fear of becoming the poor Hispanic girl from East LA who never amounted to anything was coming true.

I became obsessed with training for the Boston Marathon. In order to qualify, I had to run 26.2 miles in three hours, thirty minutes, and eight seconds. I gave myself six months to achieve that time. Running the Boston Marathon was something anyone would be proud of! It gave me a goal and distracted me from the fact that I didn't have a job, and I didn't know what I was going to do with myself. Since I trained with a running group that was training for the LA Marathon, I figured I may as well run that too. I shaved time off my runs and eventually ran twenty-five miles in three hours, fifty-eight minutes, and thirteen seconds. I figured cropping another measly twenty-eight minutes would be a piece of cake. (You know this setup isn't going to turn out well for anyone, right? I now know that runners train their entire lives to get Boston-ready, so go ahead—side-eye me. I was on my way to run my fastest marathon yet.)

Face Your Fears Instead of Running from Them

We arrived at Dodger Stadium at 5:00 a.m. on race day (March 20, 2011). The route was known as the "Stadium to the Sea." I had trained to run outdoors without music because I wanted to be alert, but I figured the marathon would be my best opportunity to run *with* music since the hazards were minimal. I was in the zone. I had done everything I could, and I knew if I was going to get anywhere near my Boston goal, I'd have to start slow. My mantra was "slow and steady wins the race." If I went slow in the beginning, I could pick up my pace toward the end. Slow meant "don't gas out within the first few miles." I remembered my yoga teachers who would say, "How you do everything on the mat is how you do everything in life." I knew deep inside that I was overcome by this manic person who suddenly got obsessed with winning, even though I had never won at anything in my life. I didn't care what the cost was. I figured I could go back to being yogic after the race. If yoga is about bringing the unconscious parts of ourselves front and center, this was definitely a part of me that felt unpleasant.

We'd been warned there would be rain on race day. It doesn't rain much in Los Angeles and I hadn't trained for wet conditions, but I thought, *How bad could a little rain be?* Torry and my bestie, Autumn (my ride-or-die), chauffeured me to the starting point. A few of my running companions engaged in small talk, but I was distracted, thinking about my big celebration at the finish line. I'd convinced myself that completing the LA Marathon fast enough to qualify for the Boston Marathon would demonstrate that I had arrived and achieved a successful life. Then I could be happy.

The weather was cooler than anticipated and cooler than most of my training runs in Griffith Park. As soon as the starting bell went off, a torrential rainstorm started pouring down. Ten miles later, as we passed Los Feliz, it started hailing. Is this a sign? In Spanish, *feliz* means "happy." There was nothing feliz about what was happening.

By mile sixteen, everything started to fall apart, literally. The wind was so strong it blew the mile markers completely off the ground. The once enthusiastic sideline crowds huddled under awnings, and the course looked like news coverage of a Florida hurricane.

I knew from my previous two marathons that something happens at mile sixteen. Your body is already in as much pain as it's going to be in. Everything hurts; *everything* hurts. If you're thinking, *Why would anyone sign up for this?*, here's why: some people get tattoos, some jump out of airplanes, some shop, others eat mushrooms. I run. I remembered the quote, "The mind will give up one thousand times before the body will." I wondered if the guy who said that had ever run a marathon in a storm.

All the mile markers past mile eighteen were *gone*, and I relied on my watch's pace-time estimations to gauge how far away the finish line was. Ambulances lined the streets, tending to runners with hypothermia, and conditions were getting worse. I was *not* going to stop. I went from channeling my best motivational quotes to cursing the day running shoes replaced my meditation cushion. I missed that moldy carpet from my first meditation practice now. I was in pain, soaked, and freezing but emphatically determined to finish this thing. I could do this! "SLOW AND STEADY WINS THE RACE." I'd grown up in a neighborhood with gang violence. I'd avoided going to jail. I'd witnessed armed robberies, drive-by shootings, our neighbor getting stabbed. Running in this storm was *nothing* compared to all that.

I was shivering, my breathing was shallow, and I was tripping over my own feet as exhaustion and hypothermia took hold. Barely anyone was left running on the street. I thought about everything that had happened to bring me to this moment, in the middle of this storm, which felt like an external manifestation of what was happening in my life. I'd achieved a place in life where other people thought I'd made it. Then I blew it up. I was afraid of what my future was, because I couldn't see it. I chose to run from my fears instead of facing them. I wasn't enough for myself; I wasn't enough, period. I would never live that happy life I had at one point dreamed of.

I thought of my parents. When they separated, my dad would stay up all night, crying, lamenting his broken heart, wishing he had done things differently. I wondered if I would have the same regrets if I chose to leave my seven-year relationship.

I looked at my watch and clocked my time. I'd already been running for more than four hours. I wasn't worried about my Boston time anymore or the fact that I was slipping into hypothermia. I was getting closer to the ocean and estimated I was at mile twenty-five. I could see a mile marker off in the distance, and I repeated my mantra, "Slow and steady wins the race." I was emotional, and the plan had been to suppress all emotions until after the finish line, maybe even until I got home, so I could cry in private. With that plan blown to hell, my new plan was to never run for the rest of my life. I finally got close enough to read the mile marker clearly. It read **MILE 22.** Have you ever had that happen to you? You think you are at the end of a project or a goal, and then *BOOM*, life punches you in the face.

A stream of tears rushed down my face. All the feelings. A runner came up next to me and kindly asked, "Are you okay?" to which I responded through broken sobs, "I'm fine." *I'm not fine.* He asked if I needed an ambulance, but I pulled it together and said, "No, I'm okay. I'm just upset, but I think I'm okay." *I was not okay.*

On Sunday, March 20, 2011, the Los Angeles Marathon's storm was reported as the worst weather in the race's history.

The puddles were so deep they submerged our feet and thousands had to be evaluated for hypothermia, myself included. But I finished. I crossed the finish line.

The ride home was quiet, and I wondered if Torry and Autumn thought I was a running fraud because I didn't make my time. Torry prepared my ice bath and I got in the tub. He was quiet, as was I, and he knew something had happened to me during my 26.2-mile journey. I sat in the ice quietly, staring at my frozen legs. He went into the bedroom, grabbed his red plaid Pendleton jacket, and placed it over my shoulders. He leaned in, kissed me on the forehead, and said, "You made it, babe. I'm proud of you." He headed toward the door as I took a deep breath.

I closed my eyes. "I made it."

I remembered something I'd heard in one of my teacher training sessions. Our teacher quoted Mark Nepo discussing how salmon make their way upstream. Salmon move through streams by bumping repeatedly into blocked pathways until they find where the current is strongest. Strong currents present fewer obstacles and although it's the hardest way to swim, the path is clear. Maybe running was the only way I could move through the fear I was facing. Running was my way of proving to myself that I could *fail forward*. Instead of running from my fears, I was compelled to face them. It showed me that I was resilient, that I could bend, and that I could go back to the beginning. After all, don't we all start from rock bottom?

We are all winners. We've all won the most important race of our lives. Our life. In Suzy Kassem's poem "Remember Your Greatness," she writes, "You won the race for life / From among 250 million competitors. And yet, / How fast you have forgotten / Your strength, / When your very existence / Is proof of your greatness."

Be Willing to Learn

I learned that even if you *can* go fast, you *will* slow down at some point. If you don't do it on your own, life will do it for you. This is an opportunity to build a unique strength. Hindsight is always 20/20. Now I look back and think, *Why didn't I just enjoy my twenties instead of wasting so much time being insecure?*

Look back at your own life to the moments when you demonstrated your own unique strength and resilience. You can find moments of contentment and happiness, even when you're in the middle of rebuilding yourself. What if you are in the middle of a breakdown right now? If/when you break down, you can fill in the gaps and rebuild with gentleness. Focus on being steady, open, and balanced.

In yoga, each posture should have two important characteristics—stira (steadiness) and sukha (sweetness or "good space"). The steadiness grounds you in the present and gives you a stable foundation. The sweetness or "good space" lets you remain open. One of the main goals in teaching a balanced yoga class is to guide the student to achieve a state of homeostasis. Homeostasis comes from the Latin *homeo*, which means "similar." *Stasis* means "inactivity or equilibrium." Being steady/still is the foundation for creating more balance.

I felt great for months after my marathon disaster. I took time off from running since I didn't know if crying while I ran was going to become a regular thing. Not achieving my goal time was a gift. I spent time in open spaces, and with people older and wiser than me. It takes a lot of effort to run from your fears, to avoid conflict, and to not speak your truth. It's even more work to stay in motion, to do things quickly at a hurried pace. What's the rush?

I learned that happiness is not an external quest. It's not hiding in the next big purchase, relationship, or career move. Happiness is never found in the waiting. It's found in **committing** to your resilience. I made a vow to stop wasting precious time by postponing, worrying, or waiting for the world to stop for my perpetual uncertainty.

> *Happiness is never found in the waiting. It's found in* **committing** *to your resilience.*

Happiness ebbs and flows like waves in the ocean, or ripples in a lake. I'm not happy if I'm not improving, evolving, moving

YOU ARE RADICALLY RESILIENT

forward, and learning. I acknowledge that regardless of the goal, it's the process that creates resilience. That's what's most valuable, not the result. Pay attention when you catch yourself thinking, *My life would be better if____; When I get____, then I'll be happy;* or *If I could just____, then I'll be happy.* The mind always wants what is better. If you remain open to learning, and forging ahead, you will find long-lasting happiness.

I AM RADICALLY RESILIENT NOW

Here are some chapter takeaways to help you feel your own unique strength and happiness.

1. **You must support yourself:** Acknowledge that you may have a belief that isn't serving you. Develop an open mind to learn a new way of being that will serve your unique strengths.
2. Face your fears, don't run from them.
3. Recognize that you are already resilient.
4. Each disappointment carries a lesson.
5. Affirmation: ***Bring to mind a situation where you felt yourself bounce back, a time you were able to bend. Repeat the affirmation "I am radically resilient, I will bend, but I will not break."***

Journaling Exercise: What Is Slowing Your
Growth?

How do we surrender in order to let go of the past?
Follow these steps for reflection, writing, and taking
action:

1. **Take responsibility for inertia and habits that
   aren't serving you.** Relinquishing responsibility
   and waiting for someone to rescue you are signs of
   inertia. You've purchased the course, hired the
   therapist, employed the teacher, or recruited a
   friend to be the one who saves you or does the
   work for you. They won't. Expectation is premeditated resentment. This is a dangerous place to be
   because resentment won't take you out of inertia or
   stagnation. Realize this—no one is coming to your
   rescue. You have to take responsibility for yourself.
   Begin by exploring the pockets of your life in which
   you are not fully awake. This can show up in certain beliefs or expectations you have from others.
   Consider where inertia is playing a role in the situation you are currently in. Create a list of five
   things you are waiting to accomplish and haven't.

2. **Dig a little deeper.** Excavate the symptoms and causes of your stress. Most of the time the source that you *think* is causing you stress isn't really the *root* of the stress. Ask yourself, *What are the causes that I routinely blame for my stress?* Then ask yourself, *What is the **real** source that is holding me back?* People will disappoint you. People will rarely live up to your expectations. Don't try to change anyone but yourself. How are you willing to show up for *you?*

3. **Self-inquiry: Why are you seeking what you seek?** Once you've gained clarity over what has been obstructing you, you can conquer inertia by asking yourself: *What is my sense of truth? Am I seeking emptiness or fullness, and why?* Is your reason for seeking emptiness or fullness truly authentic, or is it a way of hiding from the truth?

This process of self-inquiry will help you create more discernment, achieve more clarity and a luminous sense of understanding, and, ultimately, create the momentum you need to find more fulfillment in your life. You'll stop stepping into the same potholes and ultimately understand why you are here.

When we arrive at the moment where we can unhook ourselves from past experiences, put in the required effort, and get clear about what we want, we can achieve emotional freedom. What prevents us from reaching our goals is that we act out from the past unconsciously. We constantly travel with our past then resent that we brought it along in the first place.

My prayer for you is that you avail yourself of resources that remind you to practice and surround yourself with support. You know it's going to be work, but you have the capacity to remain vigilant and hopeful and deeply moved by those around you and to know at a deep level that you are radically loved.

Essential Tips for Running as a Self-Care Practice

1. **Make a training schedule:** Keeping a schedule or running log helped keep me on track and it was key in helping me slowly build to run longer distances.

2. **Gear up:** Having the right type of running shoes can make all the difference between having a good run or having your running career end after the first lap. It's important to do the feet-to-head check: shoes, knee guards (if you have sensitive

knees), waist belt for water, running watch to keep your time/mileage, and a hat if you run where there is lots of sun.

3. **Train with a friend:** It's always better together. Having a running buddy is a great way to stay motivated. You can help build each other up, as we can sometimes fall into laziness.

4. **Run/walk ratios:** Doing run/walk ratios helps with your recovery. Start with 4:2: a shorter run for four minutes, then walk for two minutes. Then build to 5:1, then 6:2. I've run four marathons, and I've used a run/walk ratio through the entire training and actual races.

5. **Outdoors:** Running studies have shown that outdoor running increases leg strength and ankle flexibility more than treadmill running. Plus, it's a great opportunity to get some fresh air and connect with the elements.

6. **Yoga:** Stretching before and after a run improves recovery. Postures like Warrior I, Warrior II, Supta Padangusthasana (reclining hand-to-big-toe pose), Trikonasana (triangle pose), and Janu Sirsasana (head-to-knee pose) help develop strength

in the core, quads, hamstrings, and hip flexors, which create the stability needed to keep you injury-free.

7. **Roll your feet:** I suffer from plantar fasciitis. Use a tennis ball to roll the bottoms of your feet before and after you run. When rolling, move from side to side as you roll the ball from the toes to the heel, making sure to cover the entire sole of the foot.

8. **Hydrate:** Being dehydrated can prevent you from having a good run. As you sweat during your run, the volume of blood in your system decreases so you have less pumping to your heart. This results in less oxygen-rich blood for your muscles. Your energy gets bogged down and you slow down as a result.

9. **Meditate:** Meditation pre- or post-run is a great way to keep you motivated. It's also a great way to keep you in the present moment. You can also use your run as a meditation and to practice mindfulness. Simply take in as much detail as you can, focus on your breath, connect with your surroundings, listen to sounds, and feel your entire body working in unison with the environment. Try

my Meditation for Runners at www.radically loved.com.

10. **Get plenty of rest:** Try a Yoga Nidra. *Nidra* means "sleep." It's a meditation you can do lying down, like Savasana. You release tension and go into a state of relaxed present awareness. It is one of my favorite things to do the night before I go for a run. Try my recording Yoga Nidra for Runners at www.radicallyloved.com.

CHAPTER 7

YOU ARE RADICALLY GRACEFUL

Radical Truth: Take a chance. When in doubt,
remember who you are.

For Halloween when I was in the second grade, I dressed up
as a ballerina. I was twirling around on the grass when my
teacher told me to stop it because I was too "ungraceful." Anytime I heard the word *grace* after that, I knew that whatever it
was, I didn't have it. It took some unlearning to discover what
grace truly meant.

When we buy into others' beliefs about what we *can* and
can't do, we prevent ourselves from healing, growing, and living
our best life. The same goes for when we try to apply our ideals
onto what we *think* someone else *should* be doing. We need to
MYOB (mind your own business). Focusing on what someone
else believes about us creates blind spots that keep us from

seeing our true oneness and grace. It causes us to suffer. We are fragile and can be easily swept away by self-doubt and insecurity. We need to have compassion for others and ourselves so we can let grace in. Compassion means you are aware of the suffering of others. Self-compassion means you are aware of your own. It means being aware of your internal pain and having a desire to understand it. When you practice self-compassion, grace enters where it already abides.

Grace differs from resilience in that resilience is something we acquire and grace is something we let in. We aren't born with resilience; we grow to be resilient. It grows into a skill set that improves and strengthens over a long period of time. The more resilient you are, the easier it is to be gracious. Grace, on the other hand, is the ability to feel loved just as we are, so we can love others just as they are.

Before I got kicked out of catechism class, I was taught that there are two types of grace. One was Sanctifying grace, and the other was Actual grace. Sanctifying grace is perennial; it resides in the soul. Actual grace is spontaneous. Both can provide inspiration, insight, or the confidence to act. In essence, Grace is to be radically loved.

I taught yoga classes, went to school, started therapy, and attended frequent AA meetings with a friend who had relapsed. It was much easier to practice compassion toward others than to have compassion for myself. I became very good at helping others hold their pain and suffering, but I neglected my own. I became good at helping other people solve their problems while not being honest about my own.

Grace and Relationships

One of the most important things you can do for your health is to mind your close relationships. Determine whether they nourish or deplete you and know when it's time to move on. It's difficult to break up with friends or family who aren't on the same healing path. Relationships that no longer serve you, however, don't always have to end on bad terms or a breakup. Some of your people may be inspired by your growth and decide to do some internal work themselves. Other times, you need to put space between yourself and those you've outgrown. In yoga, we look at everything as having prana—vitality or life force. We are either nourishing ourselves with prana or depleting ourselves of prana. Relationships that serve your highest good make you feel supported, empowered, and inspired. These are prana filling. They're like adding water to a glass.

Relationships that leave you tired, uninspired, and a little bit used are prana depleting, like water getting siphoned out of a glass. We've all experienced relationships ending, and we often find ways to avoid doing the hard things that need to be done.

We'll ghost people or pretend to be busy so that we don't have to engage. We do what we need to do to survive energetically. We must be mindful of our energy because anything can become a source of depletion. What's medicine for one is poison for another.

Some relationships both nourish and deplete your prana, and that is especially difficult when it happens in a romantic relationship. I felt like Torry resented how much time I spent doing internal work while he was busy trying to figure out how to financially support us. He was concerned about our livelihood and I was concerned about our fundamental communication issues and the fact that he had no spiritual practice. All concerns from both parties were equally important.

I was unable to practice self-compassion, so how did I expect to have compassion for the person I loved the most? We were on two completely different paths. Instead of giving our relationship space and acknowledging our pain, I became reactive and closed myself off. People are afraid that receiving grace and compassion when we make mistakes will stop us from improving and growing. That is rarely the case.

Self-compassion guides us on our journey toward transformation by removing our fear of failure, which often stops us from opening. We can be radically honest with ourselves and still be in a state of power. When we respond to ourselves with compassion and radical love, we acknowledge that what we want in our mind and our actions are contradicting each other; e.g., you want peace, but you're not acting like it. Just be honest with yourself.

I resented that I was on the spiritual path and Torry wasn't. I believed if he was on the spiritual path, he wouldn't be so worried about us potentially losing our home. I would leave books on his nightstand and play audiobooks in the car when we were together, hoping that he would hear something that would give him some respite and a different perspective. This only caused him more stress. I sent invites to his calendar for yoga classes, workshops, and resources for therapy. But all he could see was that I was not happy.

We had "nothing conversations" every day—the kind you have with your partner about a specific issue that renders no solution. The kind where you talk in circles, repeating the same things because neither of you is listening.

You can't force anyone to be spiritual, just like you can't force anyone to, say, like a particular ice cream flavor. If you want to change someone's mind, you can either be an ambassador or a recruit. Ambassadors will take you through the entire ice cream experience—the flavor's uniqueness, notes, and texture. Their authentic approval creates a natural curiosity within you and maybe you try this new flavor. Recruits are militant, like my probation officer, a Korean war vet. A recruit will lecture you about how every single flavor of ice cream you've tried in your life was wrong. This flavor is the one you've been missing, and your life will forever be incomplete without it. I was a recruit, and just for the record, recruits won't listen to whatever you have to say. They tell you what to do rather than show you a different way. In addition, being a recruit is the worst way to convince someone to change. Sometimes you need a recruit, but other times, you need an ambassador. Discernment determines which is best.

This went on for a year. We were tired of battling each other. It was difficult to sleep in the same room, and in a short period of time we knew that things needed to shift or we were done. At the time, we were living in Laurel Canyon. We hadn't paid the mortgage in over a year, and we knew we would have to find a new place to live. Torry grew up in Oregon and thought we'd have a better quality of life somewhere outside of the LA machine. Portland was a short two-hour flight from LA and was more affordable for us.

Even though LA had brought me so much heartache, it was all I knew. I didn't want to leave, but I knew that for us to shift our perspective, we had to get out of our environment. We needed a fresh start in a new city. I was submerged by the familiar doubt that crept in any time a big decision needed to be made.

Autumn and I were having lunch one day, and she graced me with some sage advice: "If it doesn't work, just come home." Even though I wouldn't have a home to come to, I knew she was right. That gave me the comfort I needed to agree to move. In *The Yoga Sutras of Patanjali*, the practice of nonattachment is vital. Not every decision has to be etched in stone. We can change our minds, try something on for size, and if it doesn't fit, move on. We had a big moving-away party. Our friends showed up to wish us well on our journey and told us they would be there when we decided to move back.

We packed up our LA home, plus our two French bulldogs and Chúy, our newly rescued shih tzu, and prepared for a sixteen-hour drive to our new city. While Torry played Tetris with boxes in the sixteen-foot moving truck, I loaded Chúy into my car, pulled out of the driveway, and waved goodbye. We would drive to our new home separately.

I got as far as the bottom of our street before I burst into tears. As I snaked through traffic on Laurel Canyon Boulevard, I lamented to my dog, "This is the last time we'll ever drive down this street, Chewbug."

Chúy looked puzzled, curled up, and plopped down on the passenger side—a dog's way of practicing nonattachment.

I went back and forth in my mind about the pros and cons of making such a big move.

Doing Hard Things

I was at USC General Hospital, and I went to school, met my life partner, and went to work all within an eight-mile radius of the hospital where I was born. I'd never driven by myself for longer than five hours. Being alone for a cross-state drive was unnerving, but knowing that Torry was only an hour behind me made me feel safe-ish.

I listened to Brené Brown's audiobook *Daring Greatly* as I drove north to Oregon. She spoke with subtle Texan inflections, and I responded aloud as if she were speaking directly to me. As I drove and listened, I cycled through excitement, sadness, rage, curiosity, and fear. The fear set in somewhere near the Oregon border.

I tried to focus on positive thoughts. Just then, Brené Brown began reciting a quote* by Theodore Roosevelt:

> The credit belongs to the (wo-)man who is actually in the arena, whose face is marred by dust and sweat and blood; who strives valiantly; who errs, who comes short again and again, because there is no effort without error and shortcoming; but who does actually strive to do the deeds; who knows great enthusiasms, the great devotions; who spends (her- or) himself in a worthy cause; who at the best knows in the end the triumph of high achievement, and who at the worst, if (s-)he fails, at least fails while daring

---

* Adapted to be more inclusive.

greatly, so that (her or) his place shall never be with those cold and timid souls who neither know victory nor defeat.

That's when I noticed my iPod hadn't been charging and was almost out of battery. So was my phone.

It began raining as I arrived in Medford, Oregon. Torry and I had been checking in with each other, and we decided to stop there for a bite. I needed a break. The rain had been pouring down in torrents, and visions of the LA Marathon storm were surfacing. Big rigs raced by, covering my windshield with a sea of water that made the road lines barely visible. I glanced at my phone to see where I was on the map. No reception. My iPod was dead, and my dog and I were both crying. This was it. This was the end, I was going to die in a terrible car accident with my dog on my way to Portlandia. I survived living in East Los Angeles during one of the deadliest times in LA history, but this was how it was going to end.

When we got to our designated stop, Torry was already there. The moving truck had left him stranded a few miles back, but he managed to get there before me. He rushed over to see what was wrong, and I let him have it. I blasted him with all the ways he'd feel bad when something terrible happened to me. "I CAN'T DRIVE IN THE RAIN! NO ONE FROM LA CAN!" I was driving the road of death because of him, and everything was his fault. I didn't even want to move! The truth about how I felt began pouring out. All my fears, all the ways I felt unseen and unheard. He listened intently, until my cycle of rage was complete. He helped me back to my car and drove in front of me until we made it to Portland at 4:00 a.m. Over the next few days, he was able to speak his truth as well. We both listened and reflected. One of the biggest ways to show self-compassion is to express yourself fully.

We are resilient. We can withstand an unmeasurable amount of emotional wear and tear. If you honor that, you can be radically honest without fear. My biggest fear was that telling Torry the truth would end our relationship, and it did. The relationship we had pre-Portland was over, but that created the space we needed for the new one to begin.

Radical Honesty

When you can be honest about your pain, and you respond to yourself with self-compassion, pain heals. One of my teachers told me that "mindfulness is rooted in self-compassion." If we are unable to have self-compassion, then being present will become unbearable. It will be like *Groundhog Day* minus the happy ending.

We spend a lot of time distracting ourselves from the pain of life. We believe that life is hard because we are doing something wrong and it's our fault. If we see other people living their "best life" and we aren't, it's because of us. We then go down the rabbit hole of all the "shoulds": *I should be doing* ____, or *I shouldn't have done* _____, and *Maybe I should just* _____.

To move past that negative-response loop, be honest with yourself. If you realize you are doing something that's out of alignment, have some courage and give yourself the self-compassion you need to gracefully move past it. To ease into it. Remember, you are resilient. Take a chance to do things differently. When in doubt, remember who you are and that you are radically loved.

Being honest can bring forth a reality that might be hard to face, but you don't have to do it alone. Being honest can be supported by your loved ones. If we are too weak to hold up the mirror, someone else can do it for us. The truth is, life is hard for everyone. When we are honest and treat ourselves with compassion, grace enters and healing begins, though it might not look like you thought it would.

Early in our relationship, Torry and I attended a ballet performance by the Alvin Ailey American Dance Theater. Alvin Ailey was a prominent choreographer who created a multiracial modern dance ensemble to bring African American dance to all audiences. When you are in the presence of grace, even if you don't feel it, it can't help but pour into your empty glass. When I saw the level of grace, soul, and beauty integrated into movement, I finally got it. Ballet represented the ability to do something with ease, to glide through with strength, but without force. My second-grade teacher was wrong. Don't ever let someone stop you from dancing; be the ballet dancer who gracefully takes and keeps the spotlight.

I AM RADICALLY GRACEFUL NOW

Here are some chapter takeaways to help you feel graceful.

1. **You must support yourself:** Allow grace to enter and consider evaluating old beliefs that weren't placed there by you, and how you would see things differently without them.
2. Be patient with yourself; acknowledge your pain.
3. Practice radical honesty.
4. Practice self-compassion and compassion toward others.
5. Affirmation: *Place your hand over your heart. Repeat the affirmation "I am radically loved and receive grace fully."*

Moving Practice and Affirmation

Yours doesn't have to look like mine.

No one loves feeling uncertainty. In fact, most people do whatever they can to create a level of comfort, sometimes at the expense of moving forward. Here are a few ways to nourish yourself energetically while moving with life's changes, wherever they may lead you.

Replenish Your Energy

1. **Be open:** Being open can be challenging for some people. It's difficult to approach something from a beginner's mind, especially if you've spent most of your life trying to stay above water. There is a certain level of relaxation that happens when you exhale. I often think about being open as a nice, long inhale and a smooth, long exhalation.

2. **Listen to your intuition:** It's the little, wise voice that comes to the forefront of your mind or the physiological response in your body when you know something. Listen intently. This can be made clearer by making time for stillness and meditation.

3. **It's okay to not know:** We can get hard on ourselves when we don't know something that we think we should. We think we need to have everything figured out, and we need to always know what is best. That's not the case.

4. **Closer to grace:** In a moment when you feel energetically depleted, do or think of something that makes you feel joy, happiness, or grace. The mind is designed primarily for survival, not for happiness (it's okay if it takes you a few attempts). Keep it simple and focus on something outside of yourself. It could be painting, walking, writing, reading, being creative, going to a movie, going to the ballet, talking to friends, taking photos, or playing with a pet. Then allow it to fill your cup.

CHAPTER 8

YOU ARE RADICALLY HONEST

Radical Truth: What is not *expressed* is *depressed.*

talk a lot about honesty because I learned that what is not *ex-pressed* will be *de*-pressed. The reason we suffer when we aren't telling the truth is that our innate desire for expression is diminished. Truth-telling is a skill. If you don't use it, you lose it. I didn't grow up telling the truth, and after many years of trauma healing, therapy, and working with spiritual teachers, I learned that telling the truth was my superpower. It is a power we all have, and one that is vital to feeling radically loved.

In the book *What You Feel, You Can Heal* by John Gray, PhD, he discusses why it's difficult for us to be honest, and why achieving self-love is difficult. The idea is that from a young age we are conditioned to not love ourselves in five basic ways.

It's not okay to appreciate yourself.
It's not okay to desire for yourself.
It's not okay to be yourself.
It's not okay to make mistakes.
It's not okay to express yourself.

Ever since childhood, thoughts like these make us feel like we are too egocentric, too selfish, too entitled, too conditional, and too expressive. If we appreciate ourselves too much, we're in danger of being criticized by others. If you have a desire for yourself, you feel bad for wanting more than what you already have. If you are true to your own unique self, you run the risk of not appeasing everyone's expectations of you. You might learn to think that love is earned and not given. If you make mistakes, then you may lose the love that you have. If you express yourself fully, you may become ostracized by your loved ones and lose your ability to discover your potential. When you are unable to tell the truth, that results in one fundamental issue—the inability to feel loved.

When this happens in relationships, the magic you once felt begins to dissipate. No one enters a relationship thinking, *Hi, sweetheart, let's have a few years of a great communication and then become extremely triggered by everything we say to each other*, or *Honey, let's get married, and after a few years, get a divorce when we find someone better.*

YOU ARE RADICALLY HONEST

There is absolutely no way you can know if your relationship will last. The best thing you can do to keep it alive is to tell the truth about how you feel. Telling the truth in a relationship is like watering a plant. The plant is the relationship and the truth is water. What happens when you don't water your plant? It dies. I've done it many times. I didn't get the same botanical prowess as my grandmother. I am a plant killer. They come into my home all bright-eyed and bushy-tailed and in just a few weeks, even days, they are dead. Even desert plants, which I'm told are the most difficult to kill, have suffered the same fate.

Truth versus Honesty

Relationships only become complicated when you are unable to express yourself fully. Telling the truth and being honest are different from each other. If we don't like a certain truth, we are compelled to create a new one. We do this on the regular. It's what you do when someone asks you if you are okay and you say, "I'm fine." Is that the absolute truth? The truth is what lies beneath "I'm fine."

Truth is an absolute concept, and honesty is a quality by which telling the truth grows. The truth has been tested over time, and honesty is the way in which you honor that truth.

We are all masters of hiding our true feelings. We do it all the time. We do it when we fake a smile after getting an upsetting email, or when we say something "isn't a big deal" when it is. We suppress it, and after a while, it's hard to discern what is a big deal and what isn't. You begin to believe the lie, until it becomes true for you. You've then lost the truth about yourself, and in turn the ability to express what is truly happening inside. Then, when you try to express yourself, you can't.

The truth about our feelings is that they have many levels. One of the most important lessons I learned from one of my AA friends was that when you numb your unpleasant emotions, you numb your ability to feel the pleasant ones too. Everything becomes different shades of beige, and in case you didn't know, that gets tired quickly.

John Gray also talks about the warning signs that lead to the death of relationships. These signs are known as the Four Rs: resistance, resentment, rejection, and repression. Resistance is closely related to something I discussed earlier in chapter 7. I knew there was a problem in my relationship and decided that instead of facing it, I would ignore it. Most people can identify this for themselves when they feel resistant to another's feelings or what they say or do. This leads to the next *R*, resentment, which I describe as a deep level of agitation arising from something that was done, something that wasn't done, or what you predict will surely be done at some point. If you are unable to express your resentment, this automatically leads to rejection.

The accumulation of resistance and resentment causes you to not want to engage with your partner, which causes you to disconnect. If you can't express your feelings of rejection, this will lead to repression. This is the end of the line for most relationships. When you repress, you have actively achieved the numbing of all the feels. This is where it becomes problematic. See, from the outside, you may look at a relationship that has completely repressed all feelings as *Wow, they really love each other. They never have any problems*. Then boom, divorce-town! There is nothing wrong with accepting the status quo in a relationship. It's important to know the difference between accepting the status quo and being so tired of the fight that you've completely given up.

Feeling Safe

We had been living in Portland for three years when Torry embarked on his own journey (the one I had been pressing him to take for years). Crazy things happen when you give people space to live their own life and you feel safe to share the truth about your feelings. When you can be with someone who makes you feel safe and loved, whatever is repressed can come to the surface and begin to heal. He was questioning what his next evolution would look like, what he would do next. He had outgrown Portland and healed whatever he needed to heal, and he began to press me about how I'd feel about moving *back* to LA. "Wherever you go, there you are," I would say, mimicking my teachers. If you are in search of a new feeling, search here. If you are running from a feeling, then the run will continue wherever you go. One day while we were having breakfast, I finally had it with his not-so-subtle inquiries. I looked at him and said, "If you are asking me if I want to go back home, you know what the answer is."

I didn't miss the static of living in a major city, but I knew, ultimately at some point, I would end up going home. After a year, we sold our house in Portland, packed everything up *again*, and moved back to LA.

Creating Security Within

Creating security within yourself requires truth-telling. You must speak your truth and listen to whatever feelings are present. You must face your fears instead of running from them. You must practice self-compassion and give way to grace. It's difficult to tell the truth, to be honest, especially when we have old impressions manning the ship.

We've learned that we can create new impressions to take away from old ones. This paves the way for our journey to self-love. A great way to do this is to reframe the old conditioning. To know that:

It's okay to appreciate yourself.
It's okay to desire for yourself.
It's okay to be yourself.
It's okay to make mistakes.
It's okay to express yourself.

Often, what stops us from getting to that place where we feel safe is not knowing whether it will have a positive or negative effect. The reality is, we can't create false security by thinking we know everything. We don't, and there's no way of ever knowing anything for sure.

If we try to create security by "knowing everything," we take away life's magic and mystery. We close ourselves off from new experiences, new people, and new ways of thinking. Just because a situation is familiar doesn't mean you should stay in it forever. For us to create more union, we need to tell the truth, ask for help when we need it, and believe that we are radically supported no matter what. This helps us to navigate "not knowing." Even if we can't see that we are radically supported, we are. We wouldn't be here if we weren't.

I gravitated toward more contemplative practices that felt

There is no substitute for being still within yourself. open and accepting of my flawed human way of being. My spirituality practice paved the way for me to no longer feel like an outsider. I was able to be still and feel the comfort of what was present, radical love.

There is no substitute for being still within yourself. Real healing begins when you can just be alone with your thoughts. That's the relationship that is most important, and we need to create space for it. In my years of practice, I have encountered many teachers, mentors, and guides, but in the end, I have found the most healing by being still within myself.

The person who knows you the most and is with you 24-7 is *you*. You are an expert at being yourself.

Your Spiritual Practice

Spirituality or spiritual practices may include prayer, meditation, chanting, breathing exercises, rituals, and the like. It's important to learn and accept that we are spiritual beings having a human experience, not the other way around. When you're in pain, desperate for help, or in a state of disconnection, you may be willing to follow any path to get yourself out of trouble. It's easy to get seduced by spiritual practices when we are in a deep state of suffering, trying to find answers or make sense of our lives. We get confused about what is real. We may not know what we want our future to look like, but we can still practice being spiritual, connected individuals right now, wherever we are. Seek wise teachers (ones with good reputations), read sacred texts, and give yourself time and space to integrate their teachings. Seek out the truth-tellers and the honest people who have stood the test of time.

I've known many people who drink whatever Kool-Aid they are offered in the form of intelligent marketing, fake followers, and clickbait-y YouTube videos. Ask yourself how something makes you feel. If we've practiced repressing our feelings, it can be confusing to know how we truly feel. This can take time, and that's okay. What you feel, you can heal.

Your spiritual practice should feel good, of course, but its nature is to take you through places you may not want to see. Create agency within yourself so that you enter with your eyes open. Faithful, but not blind. All spiritual practices are designed to help you traverse a treacherous course. In the end, we are all equal before the cycle of life and death. Everything that has a beginning has an ending, and our spiritual practice gives us the grace we need to move through it.

What you feel, you can heal.

I AM RADICALLY HONEST NOW

Here are some chapter takeaways to help you feel radical honesty.

1. **You must support yourself:** You don't have to change everything in a day. Begin by acknowledging how you feel. Journal your feelings daily, stream of consciousness, for a set period of time, and see what shows up. Set your timer for five to seven minutes.
2. What you feel, you can heal.
3. Create security within yourself.
4. Find a support system that is honest and known to tell the truth.
5. Affirmation: *Place your hand over your heart. Repeat the affirmation "I am radically honest with myself and give myself the space I need."*

Moving Practice and Affirmation

We are constantly receiving feedback with our bodies. We can see the choices that we make, whether it's the clothes we wear, or the food that we eat. We wear our choices. Clearing our bodies from emotional and physical pollutants is key to our spiritual health. When we are not aware of our emotions, we are at their mercy; this relinquishes our ability to discern. Some of the ways we do that is by talking or writing things down, and when we feel like crying, we do that too.

Take a walk with a friend. If you can do it without your phone, even better. Discuss why you make the choices you do, without judgment, then listen to them. List the reasons you are interested in being on the spiritual path. If they are also on a spiritual path, ask them what brought them to the path to begin with. If they are not, ask them what brings them peace, and where does that center of peace live within or outside of them.

PART III

SPIRIT

Widen your aperture to let the light in.
We are subatomic particles moving
at the speed of light and therefore
are all connected.

CHAPTER 9

YOU ARE RADICALLY ENGAGED

Radical Truth: Inquire within, engage with others.

Every relationship has its ups and downs. If we ignore our relationships and think they will simply continue as they always have, then we're not paying attention. If we think things will eventually change for the better, but we don't have a plan for change, then we're not actively pursuing what we want.

Being in a relationship is among the highest forms of spiritual practice. For many of us though, when we are in a relationship and in love, we think about all the ways our relationship could be better. In contrast, when we aren't in a relationship, romantic or otherwise, we think about what it would be like to be in one. The mind always wants what seems better.

When you are first dating someone, you experience the

excitement, joy, and ecstasy of being with someone new. The butterflies in your stomach, the giddiness of getting a message from them, the excitement of being in the person's presence. Those feelings eventually fade away. The cloud of newness dissipates, and that's when you get to *know* the person. You're no longer intoxicated by the hormones coursing through your body during the attraction phase.

The beginning of relationships is really you, just experiencing *yourself.* One can sense the love, but really, the experience of love is happening within you. It takes a lot more than initial attraction to see who the other person is. You can then make a conscious choice to actively engage with that person or not.

Engaging versus Connection

Have you ever gone to a yoga class and smiled at someone but only because you don't have to engage with them? Engaging with other humans is difficult for some of us. We may not have natural friend-making abilities, or we may feel guarded about our feelings.

During my early days of practicing yoga, I enjoyed the comfort of a yoga studio. I liked *being* with people, but I didn't want to *talk* to anyone. It would be like, "Hey, I'm here, but don't talk to me, okay? Thanks. You stay in your joyful space over there on your mat, and I'll stay in my joyful space over here on mine. Then when I'm done, I'll leave without making eye contact with anyone lest I have to engage in conversation."

See what I mean?

The difference between engagement and connection is this. Engaging with someone is an **intentional** practice. If we say someone is "engaged in writing," we mean that they are making a conscious effort toward the practice of writing. If someone were to say that they were "connected to writing," we might assume that is simply a mental attitude about writing. If someone says they're "passionate" about writing, all we know is that the person had an emotional reaction to writing; not that they have accomplished or participated in the action themselves.

We can achieve connection through engagement, but we can't achieve engagement through connection. One is the product of the other. We can't say we connected to someone and subsequently engaged with them any more than we could say that we had eaten a meal and then made it. Both are important, and there's a specific sequence of events.

Growing up, I avoided eye contact with people because that could potentially put me in a bad situation. Engaging came at a dangerous cost. My romantic relationships had also not been great, so my examples of how to connect were all over the place. When we are in a relationship, engaging and connecting are a fluid dance that requires our active participation. For me, this was a scary process. What happens when you engage and connect with someone? At some point, it ends.

When Torry and I were going through a difficult time, we had to face this reality. One evening, we decided to go to Venice to have dinner at our favorite restaurant. We hadn't gone out anywhere for a long time because we couldn't afford it. When we arrived, our conversations were more pleasantries than anything. Small talk filled the space between us, so we didn't have to feel the thickness of impending doom.

There was so much I needed to say, but I didn't have the words. I had spent so much time convincing myself that everything was okay. I was in the repression phase. I didn't want to engage because I knew that if I did, we were going to have a very difficult conversation. However, my inability to express my feelings created a deep level of resentment toward him. We ate our meal and quickly headed back to the car.

We walked along the sidewalk and got to the car when he asked, "Do want to go stick your toes in the sand?"

I nodded, and we walked toward the water. I kicked off my sandals so that I could feel the tiny grains of sand between my toes. We found a spot and sat down. We sat in silence, the sky still glimmering from the passing sunset.

"You're not happy," he said, breaking the quiet. "You're not happy with me."

I said nothing. I hoped my silence would be enough to alert

him I didn't want to have a conversation. I had disengaged months prior so that I would be equipped to end it. We went home, and when we got there, I burst into tears. I didn't know what I wanted, and I was confused, angry, and full of resentment. My inability to be honest with Torry kept me from engaging with him. It was my defense mechanism. I didn't have any solutions, and truthfully, I didn't believe it would get better. That night, between feelings of sadness and a tiny sliver of hope, we decided to give our relationship another chance. To bring a relationship back to life, there must be two willing participants. You don't have to know how you are going to get there, you just must be willing to try. We both agreed to create a plan for change and proactively did what we needed to do to make it better.

Our relationship had to be broken down before we were able to rebuild. For me, giving up would have been easy. However, if I really believed everything I had learned up to that point, then becoming fully engaged with the person I loved would give us an opportunity for a deeper connection. A trust in grace, a trust in radical love. I was willing to start again from the beginning. To get to know each other as the people we currently were. To encourage each other's attempts to change as opposed to throwing our hands up in the air when we fell back into old habits. We messed up, a lot. I valued doing spiritual work, and he valued verbal communication. We started dating each other again, we made time for sharing how we felt. We built daily rituals, we respected each other. We agreed to learn as much as we could, we worked on ourselves and jointly on our relationship. This however didn't make us immune to dealing with life.

Stay Open

In the summer of 2018, my friend Sahara invited me to an Ayurvedic Panchakarma retreat with her and two other girl-friends, Tara and Alyson.

My intention was to go, get some R & R, and reset from being on the road nonstop. I had tallied a total of only four weeks at home in the two years since I'd moved back to Los Angeles. I had gone from teaching in my living room to teaching in places with stages. I taught every week, sometimes several times per day. I traveled and taught. I traveled to different continents, often in awe of how much world there was to discover. My name appeared in magazine articles. I worked with students who had Olympic medals, championship rings, and multiple homes.

I was tired and I needed a break. I had created a healthy relationship with my body and knew it was asking me to stop. The teachings say "you teach what you mostly need to learn," and I felt hypocritical having conversations with my students about "burning the candle at both ends" while I was doing exactly that.

When I got to my room, I opened my window to a beautiful tree atop the Blue Ridge Mountains as a thick fog rolled in. Even though I had this beautiful life, I still

Mere insight won't change your life.

felt like there was no way it could last. The familiarity of "When will that next shoe drop?" was always there. I learned that mere insight won't change your life. You must be proactive, and even then, things can still fall apart.

The promise of impermanence weighed heavily. I wondered how long my relationship would last. How long my dogs would live. If I would still enjoy my work in ten years. I wondered if I could continue to make new friends and still be uplifted by my old ones. There was so much unknown.

Starting Your Spiritual Journey

You need three things to begin a spiritual quest. The first is the willingness to inquire within. The second is the acceptance that sh*t happens, sometimes for no reason. It's called life. The third is a guide whose flashlight is a little brighter than your own. The first two are simple. The last one can be more challenging.

There has been a flood of yoga celebrities on social media. They post inspirational quotes and have carefully curated grids and images of green smoothies and sunsets. I saw the value of having a social media presence to engage with people outside of my physical community. I also felt the superficiality of people pontificating about "in-depth" teachings while mostly concerned with gaining followers. Here's the thing about spirituality: it doesn't happen while you're looking at someone else's life. It happens when you MYOB (mind your own business).

To me, spirituality and *being spiritual* indicate one's ability to connect with something deeper, something that provides meaning to life. It's the ability to be kind and compassionate to oneself and to others so we can move from our own I-ness to make way for union and greater understanding, and to achieve connection.

It takes a lot more than an inspirational quote to achieve a deep level of fulfillment and connection. I wondered if maybe the people posting these quotes were posting what they needed to hear themselves. Humans need experiences, which means we need to *live* our life, not cut and paste it. We live to be in the presence of life, immersed in the grit of it all. Humans engage and connect by digging into our dreams and finding the communal support to make them come true. We must go out into the world and have relationships with people in real life, not just on social media. We must engage and connect with other humans.

It's not a bad thing to follow uplifting and inspiring teachers and others on social media. Perhaps their teachings can become a doorway to a clearer path and a deeper connection to yourself. Relying only on the external experience, however, prevents us from doing the real internal work. It distracts us from being aware of our own feelings, thoughts, and emotions and leaves us feeling spiritually vacant. Like anything, the internet is a tool, not the source.

Now that you know how I feel about social media, let's talk about finding the right spiritual guide. People from all types of faiths and backgrounds have sought the guidance of wise people forever. Why? Because wise people have seen the best and worst parts of life. Chances are they've made it through and carry some battle scars. They may be able to teach you something you don't already know. They are farther down the path than you are.

A guide may come in the form of a teacher, therapist, coach, counselor, priest, preacher, or someone who you may feel has the experience you can draw from. Is a guide required? No. However, it is helpful to have the guidance of someone who is a little further into life's journey than you are. If you are looking for someone who will just tell you what you want to hear and keep you in the realm of what is known, then you aren't looking for a teacher. You are looking for an enabler.

Be careful about who you choose for guidance, especially if you're vulnerable or going through a terrible time in your life. Abuse of power has existed for centuries in teacher-student relationships. Find a true teacher, not an idol. Idolized humans have a way of shattering their pulpits. I'll leave it at that.

Early on, I wanted a teacher but didn't know what I was looking for. Any time I found someone I really admired, I consumed everything they'd written, every lecture. Sometimes I'd even attempt to be their friend. It would only take a few months before I'd become disappointed by their character defects. They would say something that was insensitive, or they'd invite their "special" students to a desert retreat to do drugs all night. This taught me two things. One, those people aren't my teachers. Two, that's not the kind of person I want to be. I was seduced by what they portrayed to the outside world, but I cared more about the type of person they were. Was this person a truth-teller? Were they honest? Were they kind and did their teachings carry over into their personal life? Our life is unchartered territory, and we need help navigating through it. That's one of the reasons I sought out teachers. One of the best questions to ask yourself when you find someone you believe will be a good fit for you is, "Will this teacher guide me to feeling empowered in my own life? And guide me toward learning to trust myself?"

The definition of *guru* is "the one who brings the light." A good teacher guides you to find clarity so you can set a clear intention and learn to discern for yourself. The real guru lives within.

The real guru lives within.

When I lived in Portland, I was studying with a prominent Buddhist teacher and author. It was the year before I started my podcast, and I had been thinking about a few ideas. Back then, podcasting was still new. I felt insecure about the idea, but I respected the teacher's opinion and asked what he thought. In true form, his response was simply "What do *you* think about it?" He smiled as I began to list all the reasons why podcasting would be a terrible idea.

I said, "Someone else is already doing it better. No one will care or listen. Someone will come for me because I express my opinion."

He responded, "That is the worst case, and if that is the case, so what? You are learning. Isn't that what you are here for?" He told me that we build our life raft with the materials of our lives. There is no high place that we get to. We use our experience to ground ourselves in everyday life. This is how we move from the looping nature of samsara. It turns out samsara is not a person, like I believed when I was thirteen. Samsara is the continuous loop of suffering. It is painful, perpetuated by desire and ignorance.

Potholes Everywhere

He was right. Everything in life is a lesson. It's part of our spiritual practice to make mistakes, learn, and move forward. Your teacher isn't always supposed to make you feel better. They are just supposed to guide you to make the best choice for yourself. A *good* teacher will say, "Hey, you see that pothole over there?" That's it. It's up to you whether you choose to run over it or get stuck in it. A *great* teacher will say, "Sometimes roads have potholes," which alerts you that you will encounter obstacles. Teachers don't have a magic crystal ball, they don't have all the answers; they are just there to let you know where they've stumbled so you don't stumble in the same place.

I have failed at many things. I think back to what I wanted when I was a teenager, in my twenties, and even in my early thirties and think, *I'm so grateful I didn't get what I really wanted.*

If there is something you really want to create, something you really want to do, you will do it for yourself, for your own reasons. It is scary to put your wishes out in the world: to ask the universe for what you dream. For me, it was scarier to never take a chance: to go into the unknown. It's in the unknown places that we evolve, grow, and connect, and where we feel radically loved.

Everything in life is a lesson.

Just as we can't do the same things and

expect different results, we also can't *think* the same things and expect ourselves to take new actions. People say they are willing to do whatever it takes to achieve self-love, or to be in a romantic relationship, or to mend a severed relationship, but they worry that changing their mind-set won't help. How can it not?

I AM RADICALLY ENGAGED NOW

Here are some chapter takeaways to help you feel radical engagement.

1. **You must support yourself:** Every relationship goes through cycles. You support yourself by being aware and being proactive at each peak and valley. If you remain engaged, it becomes easier to move through adversity.
2. Know yourself, know your worth.
3. Engaging leads to connection.
4. Spiritual practice: Inquire within, sh*t happens, find a guide farther along the path.
5. Affirmation: *Place your hand over your heart. Repeat the affirmation "I am radically engaged with everyone I love, and am radically guided by grace."*

Questions for Journaling and Reflection

1. What is the best advice anyone has given you?
2. Who has been your greatest teacher?
3. Who has been the biggest inspiration in your life?
4. Ask four friends to choose one adjective that they think of when they think about you. Gather them all and create a sentence that makes you feel empowered.
5. If you could tell a friend one thing they can do to practice self-care, what would that be? (Can you take your own advice?)

Daily Ritual: Get Off Your Phone

Being on the spiritual path will require you to get off your phone from time to time. The phone is our pacifier. Our ability to be alone with ourselves is atrophying. To feel a sense of purpose and fulfillment, however, we must be fully awake. I often think about what would have happened if I'd had a smartphone that day on the beach when I met the loving "Best Grandma on the Planet." I wouldn't have made eye contact. She wouldn't have approached me and helped me make sense of my life. How many times have you missed a sunset? A full moon? An opportunity to help someone on the street? A simple greeting that could set the tone for the rest of someone's day? You can begin first by putting your phone in a separate room when you go to bed, or leave your phone at home when you go for a walk or out on an errand.

CHAPTER 10

YOU ARE RADICALLY WISE

Radical Truth: Your heart knows only truth.

On one of my high school ditch days, I decided to take the city bus to Sunset Boulevard. I walked past the Viper Room and headed toward San Vicente Boulevard. As I crossed the street, the sign at the Whisky a Go Go caught my eye. It read, "Ignorance is Bliss." I lived my life by that motto for years. It was normal as a teenager to ignore what was present and problematic, but that motto served no one when I brought it with me into adulthood. I learned about the caustic nature of ignorance when I learned about the kleshas, which are "the afflictions of the mind," described in *The Yoga Sutras of Patanjali*. These afflictions can prevent us from healing, from feeling self-love, and embarking on our spiritual path.

Ignorance Isn't Bliss

The first affliction in *The Yoga Sutras of Patanjali* is called avidya, which can be translated as "misconception" or "ignorance." It is the foundational and root cause of the other four afflictions. Avidya comes from the origin *vid*, which is "knowledge," "reason," or "understanding." And the prefix *a* denotes wrongful knowledge, or ignorance of a situation. Ignorance creates wrongful knowledge and misconceptions about ourselves and our reality. When we operate from a place of misconception, we create stories that are rooted in past triggers and old impressions. This causes us to react in ways we may or may not understand.

It's like this: Imagine ignorance as a dusty mirror that obscures your ability to see yourself; it gives you a clouded perception that won't let you see your own truth. It's important to maintain self-compassion, patience, and honesty for us to understand all the facets of our own truth. That's how we relate and engage with others. As we've learned, this takes practice. We are flawed individuals, and we can only do our best.

Ignorance is often depicted as a single tree trunk, with all the other afflictions branching off it. Our reality is created by our experiences. The more we learn from our misconceptions, the more we grow spiritually. Experience is what separates knowledge from wisdom. Our successes and failures shape our expectations for how our lives will turn out. The tricky part is when we create an insular ecosystem within ourselves. When we become the queen/king of our own kingdoms, we neglect our ability to tell the truth and coexist in harmony with others.

When we are afflicted with ignorance, we truly believe that *our* truth is the *only* truth, and we close ourselves off from understanding other perspectives. We've learned what happens when we convince ourselves of fake truths, right? We become unable to discern. This is the most insidious of the afflictions to overcome because there is so much to unlearn. The remedy is to be open to understanding different perspectives. When we lack the wisdom to be open, other painful afflictions grow and suffering expands in many areas of our lives.

Ego

The second affliction is our egoic sense of "I-ness" and "me-ness." This is about *me*. This is *my* story. We've all had that friend whose entire conversation consists of "I, I, I" and "me, my, me" statements. Or maybe you've been that friend (I know I have, no pun intended). One of my teachers called it the state of *self-nonrecognition*. An overpowering ego compels people to be selfish, to favor one's own material and mental needs over those of others. Mark Nepo discusses this in *The Book of Awakening*: "In the ancient Indian language Pali, the word *ahamkara* means 'I-ing,' having or making the feeling of 'I.' The word *mamamkara* means 'My-ing,' having or making the feeling of 'mine.' In Buddhism, the feelings of I-ing and My-ing are considered so dangerous and poisonous that they are seen as yet another cause of spiritual disease." Nepo says that the moment we fall prey to our ego, we become distracted from what matters most.

Attachment & Aversion

Attachment and aversion are afflictions three and four. What I want, give me more of. What I don't want, give me less of. Initially I didn't see why these two were considered afflictions at all. Doesn't it make sense to want more of what we want, and want less of what we don't want? Yes and no. It's not that simple. If we're unable to discern, and we get stuck in vicious cycles, that serves no one. In the beginning, I just wanted to feel all the good things that came after practicing yoga asana. I wanted to hear a good song while I moved my body, get a good sweat in, and get high on the endorphins of being in a flow state. It wasn't until I became aware of the bubbling truths that lurked below the surface that I decided to get out. I didn't want to feel what was present. I wanted more *feeling good* and less *feeling bad*.

Attachment and aversion keep us at the mercy of what we want, what we like, and what we fear or hate. The constant back-and-forth distracts us from seeing the truth of what's really happening. We spend most of our time being reactive to our attachments and aversions rather than operating from a place of wisdom. B. K. S. Iyengar wrote in *Light on the Yoga Sūtras of Patañjali* about how attachment and aversion create imprints of pleasure and pain on an emotional level, which perpetuate the distractions that push us from one to the other. It affects our behavior and is deeply hardwired, which makes it difficult to change. When our attachment or aversion to something creates stress and anxiety on a psychological level, it leaves little room for growth.

Fear of Death

The final affliction is the fear of death. This one is the root of fear itself. In many cultures, death isn't a taboo topic. These cultures traditionally have large family networks that provide coping mechanisms. There are many rituals before and after death.

In Western cultures, death is something most avoid thinking or talking about because it causes anxiety and stress. Death was prevalent in my life at a young age, but I was still horrified by it. The thought of going to heaven was enticing, but I'd felt shunned by my Catholic home ever since I "failed to see" God touch the sacred wafer. In Eastern cultures, we are reminded of the beauty and resplendence of the soul, the "big S" Self, as opposed to the "little s" self. The Self will put forth wisdom and truth. The self is prone to reactivity, is limited, and at the mercy of its basic needs.

Fearing death is the ultimate affliction to overcome. We can pray at temples, churches, synagogues, and mosques, but truly letting go of our fear of death is a difficult task for all of humanity. Instead of being afraid of this part of the human experience, we must learn to embrace discomforts and focus on the life that is present now. Live life with a lighter, gentler touch that leaves you open to new experiences. When you are present, you can appreciate what is here and now and what brings you joy.

Gratitude is the best practice for transforming fear. When you practice being grateful, you're less afraid of taking chances. As my spiritual journey progressed, the more at ease I felt when thinking about death. Most religions believe that we are not our bodies but something greater, nonlocal, profound, and expansive. I choose to think about my spirit/soul as something eternal, not given by my "I-ness" or "my-ness."

Heart Wisdom

It's important to use discernment to understand the complicated concept of releasing fear. Fear is a mechanism of survival. It alerts our entire system to danger. In the self-help world, I often hear leaders say, "You need to be fearless." We can't and *should not* be without fear. We should learn to discern our fear. We need to move through fear to avoid becoming stuck in the mire that stunts our growth.

The biggest moments in my life when I experienced the most fear were when I experienced heartbreak. If you've experienced heartbreak, chances are you survived, even though you may have felt like you would never recover. It is, by far, the most difficult portion of our journey, but also the one that brings forth the most wisdom.

Think about relationships in your life that have been strained, then repaired. Or think about a romantic relationship that you thought was done, but came back to life. People say, "It made us stronger." Your relationships with parents, siblings, and friends grew stronger because you went into the unknown, faced the fear, and came to understand each other in a deeper way. If you've ever experienced such a miraculous encounter, you know it's not for the faint at heart. If you made it through, then you grew an understanding of what it means to truly accept your loved ones as all of who they are. You were able to keep what truly mattered at the forefront of your mind. You knew that sometimes to rebuild, we must first break things down.

It is said that the seed of the soul rests in the heart, and I believe that. We've all heard the statement, "The heart knows." There's a certain level of knowing that is beyond doubt. How do you know you love your pet? How do you know you love a parent? A romantic partner? A sibling? A child? There is no doubt. You just know.

One of my favorite quotes of all time says: "The longest journey we have to make is from our head to our heart." A kind heart is great, but kindness in everyday action is better.

How often do you get to speak from your heart? When you truly speak from your heart, what is your tone like? What is your energy like?

If I'm speaking to someone I love or someone I care about, I mind two important qualities. The tone of my voice and the tone of my energy. I ask myself if both are rooted in empathy and compassion, and if they aren't, then I give it time. I acknowledge my truth, feel my feelings, and sometimes I take a walk around the block. That is wisdom.

I've had the biggest challenges with this when breaking up with people I'd grown apart from. Have you ever experienced being on the fence about whether you should be in a relationship or not? Have you ever felt like *I'm not sure? Is this a relationship? Is it a romance? Is it a friendship? Or is it just family? I don't know if this is right or wrong.* You do the pros and cons list, and you still feel paralyzed by thoughts like, *Well . . . I've been with this person for a long time,* or *We have kids,* or *I've known this friend since I was in elementary school.* Remember the Four Rs from chapter 8? The challenge in any relationship is to know if this person is going to accept your truth and welcome **all** of who you are.

That's how you make the decision whether to stay or go. Ask yourself if the "totality *of who I am*" is fully and unequivocally welcome in this relationship. If this person wants you to exclude any part of your truth, if they want you to change something that is fundamental to your core values or beliefs, then they are not accepting all of who you are. You enter the relationship with limitations, and it goes both ways. Of course you will have differences because we are different. But our differences shouldn't limit our ability to love and accept what is. Just as you recognize your own truth, you recognize when all of who you are is welcome. For me, when all of who I am is welcome, I know it in my heart. When all of me is welcome, it feels like home.

Be Patient

To connect to the heart and release fear, we must shift from fear of uncertainty and embrace the unknown. That's the first step. When we embrace uncertainty, we begin to live fully. When I'm not connecting to my heart, I'm not living my best life. I'm not patient. I'm not considerate. I'm just involved with my mind and my own *I-ness and my-ness* needs and desires.

Patience means that there's no urgency. I'm about to get esoteric here. Time is a construct, which means we made it up. Our careers are constructs. The things we do in our daily life have all been constructed by our need for survival, or to fulfill other needs. When I worked in an office, my boss created a lot of artificial stress. He called his employees "bees" and would create an artificial level of urgency: "This needs to happen right away. Make this happen. Do it." It didn't really make us work any faster, but it did create a lot of disdain.

How many of us place artificial stress on ourselves? How many times have you made a mistake because you were rushing? Patience allows us to take a deep breath, achieve a deep level of connection to our heart, and give ourselves the space we need.

Mark Nepo says, "When I'm not directly living from my heart, when I'm not patient, I want to problem solve your pain. So, compassion means that I want to sit with you in the pain." Being in a relationship with another requires patience, compassion, and heart-centered communication.

The mind wants to solve problems because it doesn't like to be in pain. It wants to keep you safe. Think about times when you're with someone who is crying and you say, "Oh, it's okay. It's okay." Frequently, we want them to stop crying because of our own discomfort. When someone is grieving because they've lost somebody they love, our instinct is to avert or placate. "It's okay." "Just calm down." We want *them* to calm down because *we* want to calm down. Because we're feeling the surge of grief.

When we respond from a place of wisdom, we say, "I can sit in that pain with you. In fact, can I help you carry that burden? I can't fix your problems. I can't make you feel better. But I can sit with you. I can help you hold grief." That creates a deeper connection to your own heart, your own truth, your acknowledgment of being radically loved.

Just Breathe

What should you do when you're feeling lost? Be patient, do nothing. Breathe. The breath brings you back to your heart. The breath brings you back into a state of presence. Just focus on your breath.

Empathy Is Useless

I once got in trouble with a student because of something I said during a workshop. I said that "empathy was useless." I don't think she heard what came next, but I listened to her grievance. What I said was "Empathy is useless *without compassion*." The student later apologized when she listened to the lecture recording. Empathy is my ability to understand or feel your pain. So what? What good is it for me to feel your suffering? No good at all. Compassion, on the other hand, is me having a desire for your suffering to end. You need both. Empathy is empty without compassion. When we have a desire for another's suffering to end, we can sit in discomfort together until the waves pass, the tide settles, and we can continue our journey. To me, this is the epitome of being present.

I AM RADICALLY WISE NOW

Here are some chapter takeaways to help you connect with your own innate wisdom.

1. **You must support yourself:** When you are questioning a relationship, ask yourself if all of who you are is welcome. Trust that your heart will speak the truth.

2. We have five afflictions that stunt our spiritual path: ignorance, ego, attachment, aversion, and fear of death.

3. Trust the wisdom of your experience and your heart.

4. Have patience with yourself and with others.

5. Affirmation: *Place both hands over your heart. Repeat the affirmation "My heart is full of radical wisdom, and I trust my love."*

Daily Ritual: Gratitude Practice

It's easy to drown out the mind when you know how to connect with your heart. The key is gratitude. When the heart speaks it says, *Trust me. Don't trust what is happening in your head. Trust this. Trust what is present. Trust the truth of who you are, right here, right now.* Gratitude connects us to our life, our heart, and our wisdom.

We can't fully connect to what we want when we overlook what we have. Gratitude allows us to appreciate what is present in our lives. Only then can we gain clarity about what we want.

Journaling Exercise

Sometimes thinking about what we don't want is easier than thinking about what we do want. To make it easy for yourself, make an "I don't want . . ." list and write down at least ten things.

Example: "I don't want to live paycheck to paycheck" or "I don't want to be in an abusive relationship" or "I don't want to be unemployed."

Once you've made this list, create another list of actions (what you are willing to do, how you will be proactive). Write down at least ten of these.

Example: "I am working toward more financial stability and having a nice cushion for when emergencies happen," or "I am working on myself, so that when I'm in a relationship I don't expect them to fix my sh*t," or "I'm actively looking for jobs where I can grow and be part of something bigger."

Studies show that framing situations positively (what we have), instead of in a negative context (what we don't have) can increase happiness and productivity when working toward goals. I attribute a lot of my success to writing things down. I've been writing my goals down since I was six years old.

Finally, create an ideal weekly schedule for yourself. Create your ideal schedule and don't forget to include self-care: meditation, yoga, quality time with friends, and time to connect with nature.

How much of this ideal schedule can you incorporate into your daily routine, starting where you are? (Remember to start small.)

YOU ARE RADICALLY STRONG

Radical Truth: The thing that is most true
will be the simplest, most obvious thing.
This is self-trust.

This is the going to be the hardest chapter to read. I know
this because it was the most difficult chapter to write. Loss,
pain, anger, and grief are some of the biggest emotional and
visceral experiences we have as humans. They can be mentally,
physically, and even spiritually crippling. They can make you
question what the whole point of life is and whether there is any
radical love out there for you to embrace. I get it, I know what
that feels like. If we live long enough, we will most certainly
experience this. The pain of loss is unparalleled. Our mind races
with what we could've done or what we should've done in a futile effort to find meaning.

According to psychiatrist Elisabeth Kübler-Ross, there are

five distinct stages of grief after the loss of a loved one: denial, anger, bargaining, depression, and acceptance.* Denial is normal when dealing with overwhelming emotions. Ignorance is bliss after all, right? It creates a safety barrier from the distress of loss. As the numbness of denial wears off, anger sets in. We search for someone to blame or blame ourselves, and in return, we feel the need to lash out. Then we enter the bargaining stage, asking questions like *What if I could have done something different?* or *Maybe if I'd been around more?* and so on. Bargaining provides time to adjust to reality and gives us respite from the intensity of emotions. Depression is next, which is an intense sadness that affects your entire system: mind, body, and spirit. The final stage is acceptance, and this refers to the acceptance of reality. This doesn't imply that we are "okay" with losing someone; it just means we've accepted it.

For me, this process doesn't go in order. It's sporadic. I may experience anger first, then start bargaining, then arrive at acceptance and then go back to anger.

Regardless of what systems are out there for us to draw from, at the end of the day, loss is our burden to bear. No theory prepares you for walking into a room where your loved one once

---

* Newman, Laura. "Elisabeth Kübler-Ross: Psychiatrist and Pioneer of the Death-and-Dying Movement." *British Medical Journal* 329, no. 7466 (September 11, 2004): 627.

was and no longer is. Nothing prepares you for when you hear their favorite song on the radio, or when you catch a brief scent of them that permeates their belongings.

Pain is pain. Grief is grief. It doesn't matter if you are grieving a loved one, a pet, or an old life. It all hurts just the same. Memories that flood your mind make you go back to the beginning of this process over and over. That's okay. If you know what it's like to wake up and remember your loved one isn't there anymore, I am so sorry.

These are difficult emotions to move through. They migrate in unpredictable ways. Just do your best to navigate through them so that each cycle is complete. Let each revolving emotional wave wash through you as best you can.

When it flows through the mind you may think, *I could've . . .*, *I should've . . .*, or *I wish that . . .*; all thoughts to create a sense of control when feeling out of it. Grief can manifest through the body feeling heavy, like a thick, dense cloud suffocating your being. It feels like you can't breathe. Your spirit feels broken. You question God. *Why did you do this to me? How could this happen? This is not fair.* All feelings are valid, all are appropriate.

Tragedy can strike at any moment. Pain is frequently the tuition we pay for grace, wisdom, and resilience. Though we endure our pain alone, if we are lucky, we may have the support of loved ones.

Spirituality and Grief

If you've ever lost someone you deeply cared for, you know what it's like to want solace, comfort, and peace. The first time someone close to me died was during my freshman year of high school. My childhood friends Gigi and Dulce drowned in a flash flood during the El Niño storm in the fall of 1997. They were fourteen years old. We were attending separate schools for the first time since kindergarten. At first, we didn't deal with the change well, and Gigi, Dulce, and I agreed to at least walk to the bus stop together just like we had for many years. It was the year before my car theft incident. Sometimes we would ditch school, just so we could catch up, and we'd head to a wash tunnel of the LA River by San Gabriel High School. On the day of the flood, I was under the microscope for getting caught selling pot to one of my friends. It was raining so hard that my mom drove my sister and me to school. Since ditching was no longer an option, I figured I would just meet up with Gigi and Dulce after school by the bus stop.

Bad news travels fast. I heard about the accident later that afternoon. It was all over the news. The sound of helicopters and ambulances permeated the city. Five teenagers had been swept away by the fast-moving rising water. Three lost their lives. Two were Gigi and Dulce.

The first walk back to school after their deaths was agonizing. It was the first time I ever walked to my bus stop alone. I wondered if it was all just a nightmare, that I would wake up one day and they would be there. The three of us would be walking to 7-Eleven to get our berry Slurpees. I knew it was wishful thinking, and I understood the despair of all the people in my life who had experienced loss and the pain of seeing the world continue to turn. This was the root of my anger: Why didn't anyone care? How could people smile and laugh, and go to recess and eat food? Back then, there were no grief counselors at school. There was barely a mention of what had happened.

When I found an old journal years later, I found an entry during this time period. There was a lot of scribbling and in big bold letters the words "WHY DID YOU TAKE MY FRIENDS! BRING THEM BACK!" Unprocessed grief is like a dormant volcano. The volcano has been calm for centuries, but that doesn't mean it won't erupt at any time. We saw the results of this with my colorful decision-making skills.

Many years later, I was having tea with one of my first yoga teachers, Jeanne. We were talking about grief, and I asked her, "What do you think happens when we die?"

She responded without hesitation, "We go back to where we came from."

Maybe we come from somewhere out there in the Universe and our soul floats onto this giant blue rock in the middle of nowhere. When you think of it that way, we shouldn't feel bad about not knowing what to do, or how to feel.

Grace and the Unknown

My friend and mentor Tara Mohr, author of *Playing Big: Find Your Voice, Your Mission, Your Message* emailed me one day. She asked if I knew a teacher or someone who could guide meditation privately, for a dear friend of hers. She didn't elaborate much, but I volunteered to help in any way I could, and she introduced me to Grace. We got on a call and Grace shared that she was looking for someone in the LA area to meet with her sister, Maggie. Maggie, a thirty-four-year-old talented chef, had terminal cancer. Grace was unmistakably positive and willing to go to any lengths to make sure Maggie knew that no one was giving up the battle. Without a thought, I joined "Team Maggie" and I contacted her that day.

It was early spring, nearing sunset, and all the colors in the sky created patterns of light orange rays and deep reds. Grace had suggested that I "bring anything I had in my tool kit," as Maggie was very open. I brought it all, the sage, crystals, mala beads . . . all of it.

When I met Maggie and her sister, Grace, for the first time, I was struck by their warmth and kindness. Maggie swept her hand over her shaved head as she described how she was still working full-time throughout chemo. She explained that she was determined to show up as her best self, both for battling cancer and for her future.

She had been in remission for just a few months when the cancer spread to her brain. She was willing to do whatever it took to live. Maggie prepared some green tea while I laid out all my accoutrements. We began by talking about meditation and how it had created a significant shift in my connection to God or a higher power. I explained that meditation had helped me create a deep level of listening, trust, and, well, grace. Maggie was very receptive, and we sat on the floor around the coffee table. I instructed her and her sister to close their eyes if it was comfortable. Maggie struggled with keeping her eyes closed, so I reached for the purple amethyst from my bag and handed it to her to give her something to focus on—a technique that worked for me anytime I was too distracted or anxious.

We took a few deep breaths, and I waited a few moments before I said a word. There was peace and ease in our space, along with something thick and palpable—the love Grace had for Maggie. The love Maggie had for Grace. We sat there and talked for a few hours, getting to know each other, and listening with earnest attention.

In a flash I was back in my childhood, recalling the power of community, prayer, and presence. The circle of abuelas, mamas, tías, and friends who gathered and prayed for loved ones, looking for hope, respite, comfort, and love. I was always inspired by how effortlessly they showed up to pray for someone they had never met. How they would hold one another's hands, strangers at times. A genuine heartfelt desire to "be with," to hold the pain, to have a desire for their suffering to end. The common theme, sitting in uncertainty together.

It was getting dark, and I began to gather my things to make my way home. I headed toward the door where I had left my shoes.

Maggie came over, looked me in the eyes, and said, "Rosie, can I ask you a question?"

I smiled as I tried to balance myself with one hand on the wall. "What do you think happens when we die?"

The question was followed by a long, pregnant pause. I looked down at my half-dressed foot, my hand uncomfortably pressing the wall by the front door, the other hand floating in limbo. I took a deep breath and closed my eyes. I gave her a big hug and said, "We go back to where we came from."

She paused for a moment, smiled, nodded, and shrugged, then headed back to the kitchen.

I checked in with Maggie often. The following week she sent me a text message to inform me that she had named the amethyst crystal "Purple Rain" and had taken it to chemo with her as a reminder to do her meditation practice. Just a few short months later, Grace informed me that our beloved Maggie had passed.

When Grace and I finally got to see each other again, we held each other in a pool of tears.

Pain and Suffering

Anger is my default state when I've experienced loss. I was always angry as a teenager because I believed that the world was out to get me, and I wasn't going to let her come for me. It was a sad day when I realized that the world doesn't stop for anyone's grief; that there's no universal judge out there saying, "Okay, that one's had enough suffering. She can live happily ever after now." Life doesn't work that way. I was angry at the loss of life, losing people I cared about, angry about the injustices of the world. Even now, with my brand-new shiny spiritual tools, I still succumb to my most primitive reactive state: *Why is this happening? How could this happen?* Someone once said to me that God never gives us more than we can handle. That doesn't make it any easier to sit with, because in moments of pain I *feel* like even though I can bend, I may break. Having spiritual tools doesn't lessen the pain of a broken heart.

What I do know is that I am still here, and so are you.

Sometimes the other shoe drops, the wind is taken out of

your sails, and you feel like you can't go on. That is the truth. You have every right to feel the way you do. As I write this, I can tell you that in moments of pain, the only respite I get is taking the pain, an hour at a time, minute by minute, breath by breath.

When the time is right, and you feel ready, you will feel ease and the pain will transform. When we choose to get closer to a higher power, it helps us weather the storms. For some that may be the help of a community who can support in carrying a burden. For others, it's spending time in nature, seeing the beauty that exists all around us. Getting closer to a higher power could also mean reading sacred scriptures or books. Or it could be the realization that someone else has gone through the same pain you have and survived.

The reason why writing about this is so difficult is that loss is never easy. That doesn't mean you can't do it. You can. You are resilient, you are strong, and you can withstand change.

Make no mistake, your world will change. You are being asked to become more. This is the entire reason why we have a spiritual practice. You have worked diligently to prepare for moments like this, and you will ride the waves as best you can.

If we look at our pain as a storm, we can harness its qualities to understand our own grief. In a storm, a seasoned captain with an ill-equipped vessel is ineffective. A well-equipped vessel with an inexperienced captain can be dangerous. We are the captain of our own ship. The aim is to become a well-seasoned captain with a well-equipped vessel. We need wisdom, strength, confidence, patience, and a vehicle. This is how we navigate the tide with the least amount of wreckage and come out on the other side stronger.

It is often said that "to love is to suffer," which I agree and disagree with. At its core, yes, being attached to someone or something we love, we will at some point experience pain. I'd prefer to say, "to love is to live." Love will always supersede the fear of loss, though that doesn't mean it's easy. Love is the root of all life. Pain and suffering are part of life too, part of being human. When we grieve the loss of someone we love, we are trying to fit the love of two hearts into one. The pain you feel is your heart expanding to fit all that love into one heart. The totality of another. Over time, the heart will grow. That is radical love.

When in Doubt, Movement Always

The only comfort I ever wanted when I was in pain was knowing that someone out there in the world understood how I felt. Those of you who have gone through something difficult or traumatic know it can feel like a lonely planet.

My process goes like this. At first, moving through a day feels remiss. Emotions move like the sea. I go through the motions so that each cycle is complete. What we feel we can heal. Each revolving wave is moving through my mind, body, and spirit.

When it moves through my mind, I think about what I could've, should've, or wish I had done. My body languishes, and my spirit feels broken.

These are the only moments where sitting still doesn't work for me. I need to walk, dance, flail around, or go for a run. I need to move around so that the waves have a place to go. The movement allows me to catch my breath while my mind is distracted from memories and thoughts of what should have or could have been.

Being outside gives me a different perspective and a change in scenery from the movie playing in my mind. I see a rosebush, look at the trees, and even if they don't give me comfort in that specific moment, I am reminded of the beauty and impermanence of life. I move through the stages of grief.

I search for people who have gone through the same. Knowing that someone has gone through something similar and survived gives me promise that I may be able to survive too. I can draw from the strength of others.

It sounds clichéd, but time does heal all wounds. Each moment that passes removes a thin layer of sadness, until one day you wake and notice that the sky is clear, and the sun is out, and you feel peace once again. I am sorry if you are in pain, I am sorry that you may feel alone.

There is a force around you, loving you. You are radically loved.

I AM RADICALLY STRONG NOW

Here are some chapter takeaways to help you connect with your own innate strength.

1. **You must support yourself:** Moving through pain and loss takes time, support yourself by asking for help and expressing your feelings. You are on your own time line, so take as much time as you need.
2. You move through pain, not away from it.
3. We can draw from the strength of others, to become strong.
4. Impermanence is a part of life.
5. Affirmation: ***Raise both hands into the air. Repeat the affirmation "I am radically strong, and I will feel peace again."***

Daily Ritual: Moon-Gazing

If you are a stargazer, then you may have noticed that the moon changes shape each night. Some nights, the moon is narrow like a crest. Other nights, the moon looks like a bright headlight. Some nights, the moon is not visible at all. The moon has different phases, just like we do. When I was little, my abuelita used to make me draw the moon for her. It always looked the same on paper, a big uneven circle representing the full moon with holes inside like Swiss cheese. Ever since then, I loved drawing moons on everything. Every night, I go out whether it's visible or not. I see if I can notice any differences and subtleties. I marvel for just a few moments, then I go to bed. It creates a deep grounding resonance. This powerful sphere that rules the ocean waves can coalesce with the internal waves that we can't control.

CHAPTER 12

YOU ARE RADICALLY LOVED

Radical Truth: The moments that are good and true are signs of the divine.

One morning during my meditation, I was overwhelmed by a deep sense of comfort. There was nothing complex about what I was doing, I was just listening to the sounds of the birds outside my window, when suddenly, I sensed a gentle wave of peace. I was relaxed. I wasn't engaging in anything other than what was happening in my body. I took a deep breath, which my body held comfortably. I wasn't compelled to make lists or analyze my latest Netflix binge. There was no tension, no pain. Then, in one second, my blissful moment was abruptly interrupted by my desire to laugh.

I began to think of my to-do list, and I engaged with the normal narratives that came and went: *I need to go to the grocery store*, and *I should do nothing and stay in bed all day*. The mind wants to be anywhere else but in the present moment.

Do you know why we can't stay in that blissful moment all the time? Because change is inevitable and everything is impermanent. We practice because we forget, and practice is essential. Just because we recognize our impressions and habits doesn't mean they change. Just because someone is on the spiritual path doesn't mean they have all the answers. We all search for the answers that lie outside ourselves to find the truth within us. We are all on the path because we are all trying to be better and know better—to feel radically supported and radically loved. To feel the presence of something bigger than us, we need to stop long enough to integrate it. Spirituality is something that leads us to feel connected to something greater, something that we are, and something that provides meaning to our lives when we are helpless and hopeless. This takes time. When life hits you in the face, you'll want to hit the fast-forward button. But the truth will still be there, ready and waiting for you to bring it to the surface.

Perspective

Does being a spiritual person mean you quit worrying about everything going wrong? No, but it does make it easier to cope.

Does being spiritual make life less hard? No, but it gives you the strength to go through the motions until one day life feels less chaotic. Will being spiritual make it easier to deal with loss? Well, no . . . not in the very moment you are in pain. Eventually though, it will, and it does. I know this for a fact because nothing lasts forever. The gift of impermanence. Everything you need for your spiritual journey is right here, right now, in this perfect moment. YOU. ARE. RADICALLY LOVED.

I believe there is a force greater than myself that will always bring me back to the core of who I am. A force that will transform my pain, even when it doesn't adhere to my time line. Feet on the ground, eyes straight ahead, and arms outstretched to the heavens. I can rest knowing that everything is part of a bigger vision, a vision that I may not be able to see at times. I can rest, knowing that I am radically loved and radically supported. This knowledge is as deep as the sea and as real as the sun. The journey up the mountain begins with a single step.

If you are mindful about how you navigate your journey, you can move with less rigidity. If you take it one step at a time, and appreciate each step for what it is worth, you become fully aware of your surroundings and see the landscape ahead. However, if you are only focused on the peak, you may get discouraged. You may decide the climb is too much work,

The journey up the mountain begins with a single step.

you may fall off track or quit halfway through, and that's ok. Anything worth having takes time.

We will all absolutely lose sight of the path before us, at least occasionally. Life is demanding, frenetic, and tiresome. But we can choose to pause and be still, to regroup, reorganize, and start again, and again, and again.

You are not alone. Many of us are struggling through the same life issues, fearing the same fears, enduring the same tragic losses. The world will not stop for our grief or console us when we feel lost. We can, however, choose to rise, climb, surf, dance, be still, cry, indulge in sunsets, gaze into the moonlight, go on epic road trips, and see that our will and ability to choose makes us stronger. We can plant the seeds of ideas and watch them grow. We plant seeds in the same ground where we bury things—both are equal to the earth. We go through cycles of death and rebirth; we can't change that, but we can learn to accept it so that we can live our lives fully. One final story . . .

"The Mountain Will Not Kill You, but It Will Let You Die."

My in-laws live on a twenty-acre farm in a small town in the Willamette Valley, outside of Portland. My father-in-law, Papabear, and my mother-in-law, Mama P, welcomed me from the moment we met eighteen years ago, when I was twenty years old. They have been married for more than forty years and live in the same house where they raised all three of their kids.

During one of my first visits to Oregon, Mama P took me for a little drive into town. As we approached the highway, we could see Mount Hood's clear, snowcapped summit. She turned to me and said, "It's absolutely stunning today! Can you see the mountain?" It was a beautiful, crisp winter day. I was taken by all the lush trees, vast mountain ranges, and rivers. I fantasized about going hiking and exploring the mountain peaks in the distance, very *Lord of the Rings*. I had never gone hiking, but I had just read a story about two missing hikers and asked if she knew what had happened to them. "I can't imagine how scary it would be up there all night with no help, in the cold!"

She took a deep sympathetic breath, responding, "Yeah, I heard. You know, Rosie, people forget how unpredictable nature is. A lot of hikers just don't know or are totally unprepared. They don't bring enough supplies or have the right gear, or they go off trail—"

Matching her sympathetic tone, I responded, "Oh no! that's awful! I don't ever want to go up there, then. I guess we can strike hiking off my potential hobby list."

Mama P took a sip of her beverage and smiled at me. "Aww, it's not the mountain's fault. It truly is beautiful up there. The views are stunning."

I shrugged, stared out the window, and responded, "I've lived in a dangerous place already. I think I'm good."

She smiled and replied, "The mountain won't kill you, but it will let you die."

You know those moments in your life where you can remember exactly where you were when someone said something that changed your worldview? This was one of those moments. She dropped that little wisdom bomb like it was nothing.

When I was a child, I once got swept away by a massive wave. I was playing near the edge of the water when my mom motioned for me to get in with her.

"Don't be afraid," she said, as she pulled me quickly toward the deep to move past the breakers.

I was deathly afraid of the ocean. It was big and I was small, and I didn't know how to swim. She held both of my extended arms as we traversed the shallow edge, while I unsteadily resisted to stay close to the shore. Suddenly, a large wave caught us off guard and pulled us into its revolution. I flailed and gasped for air, the ocean filling my lungs. My mother's arms reached for mine as we both tumbled through the tide. When we made it back to the shore, I refused to go back in. She said if I didn't get back in, I would always fear the sea. I didn't care. All I could see was the ferocity of the waves crashing, while I sat paralyzed with the panic that I could drown. Ocean water came out of everywhere for the next several days. I don't remember what prompted my love for the ocean after that. I don't remember how long it took, or what my process was. Maybe it was after my encounter with the "Best Grandma on the Planet." The closer you stay to the shore, the more likely you are to get pummeled by the surf; the deeper you get, the easier it becomes to swim. It's the in-between that is dangerous and uncertain. It's not the mountain that will kill you, it's the indecision of not knowing where to go, or how to climb.

No spiritual practitioner is safe from falling. The climb and the fall are both opportunities for growth. There are certain lessons we learn from our successes and certain lessons we learn from our failures. It's important to, as Kendrick Lamar says, "Be humble." The more we can lean into humility, the more the truth of our life reveals itself. We've all failed at some point or another, but we are here, as present as we can be, preparing for that climb as best we can.

We can learn humility by letting go of what we think our life *should* look like (which always presents so much better in our minds than in real life). When we take stock of our life and become truly grateful for what we have, we practice humility. Then we can discern what we want and understand that we can't just wait for what we want to come to us. Action is required. It's not going to just show up at your door. You can't order it on Amazon. (Not yet anyway.)

Ego or selfishness can cause us to lose sight of what matters.

Yogis believe that the mind and body are temporary, so we do our best to remember our true nature. Our spirit is constant and therefore is our truest self. Selfishness is the opposite of love. It creates a deep emptiness, a separation, and a lack of understanding of one's own worth. When we disconnect from our true nature, the ego controls our life. Selfishness then blinds you to the radical love that surrounds you in every waking moment. It can distract you from the simple pleasures of enjoying your morning coffee, the subtleties of a gentle kiss from your beloved, the excitement of a message from a friend, or from simply enjoying the sun, the moon, or the brilliance of the night sky. The more we can inquire within, the more the truth of "who we really are" becomes integrated. The way we free ourselves from all the afflictions is to realize that life is temporary and so are our thoughts, our pain, our to-do lists, and our astrology charts. We are here on this planet, living life, together.

Being of Service

One of my favorite definitions of *grace* is "God's unmerited favor, love, or help." Achieving our deepest desires for love, happiness, and connection typically involve another person(s). When you feel helpless, help someone. Selfless-

When you feel helpless, help someone.

ness and service bring you closer to a state of radical love. If you practice radical selflessness, ego will be abated.

I volunteered at a Skid Row women's shelter during an event my friend LaRayia Gaston was hosting. She founded an organization called Lunch On Me and authored the book *Love Without Reason*. She feeds organic meals to homeless people and curates events for the homeless where they can experience different self-care rituals, yoga, massage, reiki, and meditation. When we are deep in the throes of our own life, it's easy to forget how many people just want to be looked in the eyes and told they matter.

The final practice in this chapter is especially effective for those dealing with fear. Fear itself can be useful in the wake of specific threats, but maladaptive fear is one of the biggest problems in our world today. We're told to be afraid of so much: of not having enough, of not being successful enough, of anyone who is different from us, of having a different faith, of failing, and on and on. The truth is, when we focus on being radically loved and spreading that love through all areas of our lives, both internal and external, we become less thwarted by fear.

In the beginning of this book, I shared that I am an incessant worrier. Many people spend a lot of time worrying about things that never happen. That's usually because they've stopped focusing on what they want and who they really are (radically loved beings) and let doubt creep in. Radical love, like everything else, is a practice.

In the event of a drop in cabin pressure, you must secure your own oxygen mask before you can help others. The practicality of this is hard to dispute: if you pass out from lack of oxygen while trying to help someone else, you've helped no one. Focusing on the mind, body, and spirit connection is the oxygen mask that helps you on your journey to healing. Through practice and patience, you will get to where you want to be, in time.

Now that you have done some inner work, it's time to look outward again. By working on yourself and becoming happier, you make the world happier too.

Respect

Everyone evolves at their own pace. If you want to test out how your spiritual practice is working for you, go home for the holidays. We've learned that doing internal work can be confrontational and difficult. It's helpful to lean on the people closest to us to provide a cozy place to care for ourselves. Just because you are ready to start climbing your mountain doesn't mean everyone else is. It also doesn't mean that they aren't already on their own journey. I've had many difficult conversations with family members who are still deep in the grips of addiction. I have broken up with friends because we've grown apart and the relationship was no longer serving either of us. When I was ready to be still, I was able to listen and take more in. I told the truth; I was honest without fear of losing love. I was able to fully articulate what I wanted, even if it wasn't received with open arms. That doesn't mean you aren't radically loved.

Can we still cultivate compassion for people in our lives who have a hard time with our internal journey? It depends. Are you willing to love the people in your life, your family or friends, and accept all of who they are? Is all of who they are welcomed? Think about that one for a bit.

Discernment

Just because you love someone doesn't mean they get to take up time and space in your life. Your time and space are yours to give. Some will try to "poison the well" because you are threatening their status quo. Don't let them. Time is our most precious commodity. You can cultivate love and kindness for the people in your life who aren't on board with your growth without letting them throw you off track. It doesn't mean they are wrong, and it doesn't mean they are right. It just means they are committed to their own truth, and it doesn't allow space for yours. Empathy and compassion, self-care, and self-compassion. You have all the tools you need.

Final Note

There is no one in the world like you. You have an original fin-
gerprint that no one else has—you are not an error. You are in
just the right place. You have something special to give. Now is
your opportunity to share your love, service, time, creativity, and
expression with the world!

I'll end with a taco analogy because it is my favorite food
group. There are three types of people in the world. All three
decide to walk into a taco bar. One by one, they give their orders.
One person gets everything they wanted, and they sit and eat
their taco happily, full of gratitude, all #blessed and whatnot.
The next person gets their taco and it's wrong. They are angry,
and they replay the mistake over and over, but they sit down and
eat their sh*tty taco anyway and tell everyone it's fine. The third
person gets their taco, and it's empty. They stand there for a
second, and with a shrug say, "Hey, I'm going down the street,
there's like ten taco stands, and I want to try them all."

It's easy to believe that the only options we have are the ones
presented to us. We now know that's not the case. We get to
decide which person we want to be, how to respond, and how
to perceive the world at large. You are radically supported. So,
here's the final question. How do you feel radically loved?

I AM RADICALLY LOVED NOW

Here are some chapter takeaways to help you feel radically loved.

1. **You must support yourself:** Finding the truth of who and what you really are requires an acceptance and practice. You must do it over and over.
2. The mountain won't kill you, but it will let you die.
3. Change is the only constant.
4. Be humble, be strong, and be humble again.
5. Affirmation: *Go to a place that brings you peace. If accessible, go to it in real life; if not, go to it in your mind or use a picture. As you gaze into it, repeat the affirmation "I am radically loved. I am radically supported."*

Daily Ritual

Answer this question daily: How do you feel radically loved?

ACKNOWLEDGMENTS

This book wouldn't have ever come to fruition if it wasn't for the incredible mentors in my life who supported me and held my hand through the years. I am indebted to you forever. If your name is not listed here, it doesn't mean I don't love you or appreciate you.

To my beloved and king, Torry Pendergrass. You showed me what a radically loved life is, and I am eternally in your debt. Thank you for loving me unconditionally and accepting all of who I am.

Para mi abuelita Justa Acosta, "La amo con todo mi corazon."

My sisters. Maria "Loops" Acosta, you are my hero. Thank you for being my first mentor and for showing me what it takes to make it. Regina "Tiki-Moo-Moo" Gutierrez, for bringing a smile to my face and being my heart. You both complete me.

Toda mi familia. Mom, you are a force. I am who I am because of you. I love you. Para mi papa, por apollarme con todo sú corazon, lo amó con toda my alma. Both of you demonstrated what radical love is. Thank you. Marisol Ramos, you are the future and hope for our family.

My life-mate, Autumn Brawer, may we always look for each other, ILYSM. My sister Tanya Quintero Abriol, your loyalty and love know no bounds.

To all of my homies that keep it 100 and keep me grounded. The ones from childhood that don't want their names in this book lest the authorities are searching for them. Rosemead, East LA, Monterrey Park, Alhambra. You know who you are. Por Vida.

Eddie Veliz, my best friend and brother. Thank you for all the late nights you kept me up playing your guitar and helping me stay out of trouble, ILYSM. To the entire Montebello crew.

Hector "Lovey" Castillo, for being my first coaching client.

Sahara Rose, for giving me the support and radical love I needed when things fell apart. The true definition of #rideordie.

My literary agent, Jessica Papin, who lovingly and honestly guided me to create something I was proud of. Jeanne Faulkner, my writing godmother, for your unwavering encouragement. Marian Lizzi, for believing in this book from day one and helping the dream become a reality. A special thanks to Kelly Di-Nardo for shepherding my dream.

To Jonathan Antin, the real OG, thank you for taking a chance.

Molly Vance; my goddaughter, Naia; and Cory McCaffrey, for being my Portland family.

The Pendergrass family. My other parents, Mark "Papabear" Pendergrass and Glenda "Mama P" Pendergrass; my sissy, Piper Pendergrass-Cates; and Greg Cates. Thank you for always supporting my ideas, no matter how out there they went. ILYTM.

Cody "Buddy" Pendergrass, I would've never taken this route had you not encouraged it. Thank you for always showing up for me, without judgment. I love you, bud.

To Alexandra Kahn, for letting me teach you yoga on the kitchen floor and making me an auntie, I love you. Eli Charles Carlson, for the late-night reads and conversations that helped me structure my thoughts.

You know why your name is here. Thank you Ryan Khoo, Michael Brawer, Neeko Abriol, Lori and Earl Hightower, Eka Ekong, Chyna Chuu, Ryan Gutierrez, Henry Ammar, Michael Devin, Tara Mackey, Alyson Charles, Candice Kumai, Lisa Cron, Amberly Lago, Brant Williams, Greg Brenton, Carly and Daniel Kohn, Ryan Harris, Kelly Noonan-Gores, JD Cargill and ModPod Studio, Matt Cisneros and Backyard Ventures, Laura Brounstein, Meaghan B. Murphy, Janet Ripley, Heidi Lisiten-Krupp, Jason

Feifer, Ellen Rakieten, Heather Story, Devon Craig, Jason Low, Grace Kraaijvanger, Kelsey Meyers, Amy Morin, Kacey Janeen, Bess O'Connor, Krista Willams, Lindsey Simcik, Drea de Matteo, Danielle LaPorte, Jeff Krasno, Tara Mohr, Coach Mike Bayer, Steven Kotler, and the team at the Flow Research Collective.

To Jen Sincero and her body of work. You showed me how to be a badass.

Gina D'Orazio Stryker, for your radical love.

All the yoga teachers and mentors who guided me back home: Tracee Stanley, Tommy Rosen, Kia Miller, Elena Brower, Jeanne Heilemann, Anne Van Valkenberg, Carolina Goldberg, Schuyler Grant, Hala Khouri, and Yogarupa Rod Stryker. My Wanderlust Fest and Wanderlust TV fam.

Tessa Tovar, thank you for making the Radically Loved world go round.

My beloved and dedicated students. You are radically loved. Brenda Lynch, Lucy Li, Josie Ellerbee, Kristina Coco-Hackenjos, Ashley Domingo, Sonci Carey, Jessica Day, Melissa Mackey, Meghann Dryer, Michelle Thompson, and every single one of my students who has showed up on their mat over the years.

If I ever go missing, call Payne Lindsey.

Every single guest who has ever been on my podcast *Radically Loved*, our incredible Radically Loved community, and finally, to you. Thank you for picking up this book. May it serve your highest good.

GLOSSARY

connection: to feel completely seen, heard, and understood.

engaging: to actively and wholeheartedly participate in the act of listening.

higher power: a nonlocalized force that is greater than your self that will restore you back to health.

highest good: an action that will serve your spiritual path and is in alignment with your integrity.

present: being fully conscious of the moment and resisting the distractions from your own mind.

"secret sauce": your special, unique way of doing or saying something that empowers yourself and others.

yoga: union, to join; the practice of making the unconscious conscious.

RESOURCES

Gladwell, Malcolm. *Outliers: The Story of Success*. Back Bay Books, 2011.

Gray, John, PhD. *What You Feel You Can Heal: Guide to Enriching Relationships*. Heart Publishing, 1994.

Hart, David Bentley. *The Experience of God: Being, Consciousness, Bliss*. Yale University Press, 2014.

Patton, Laurie. *The Bhagavad Gita*. Penguin Books, 2008.

Satchidananda, Sri Swami. *The Yoga Sutras of Patanjali*. Integral Yoga Publications, 2012.

ABOUT THE AUTHOR

Photograph of the author © Torry Pendergrass

Rosie Acosta has studied yoga and mindfulness for more than twenty years and taught for over a decade. She hosts a weekly conversational wellness podcast called *Radically Loved*. Rosie has traveled all over the world leading workshops, retreats, and yoga teacher trainings. She works with a wide range of students, from those in her East Los Angeles community to Olympic athletes, NFL champions, NBA All-Stars, and veterans of war. As a first-generation Mexican American, Rosie's mission is to help others overcome adversity and experience radical love. She's been featured in *Yoga Journal*, Well + Good, Forbes, and the *New York Post*. She currently lives in the greater Los Angeles region known as the Valley.